THE CHARLES G. FINNEY
MEMORIAL LIBRARY

Evangelistic Sermon Series
- So Great Salvation
- The Guilt of Sin
- True and False Repentance
- God's Love for a Sinning World

Revival Sermon Series
- Victory Over the World
- True Saints
- True Submission

Sermons on Prayer
- Prevailing Prayer

SO

GREAT

SALVATION

SO
GREAT
SALVATION

Evangelistic Messages

CHARLES G. FINNEY

KREGEL PUBLICATIONS
GRAND RAPIDS, MICHIGAN 49501

So Great Salvation by Charles G. Finney, Copyright © 1965 by Kregel Publications, a Division of Kregel, Inc. All rights reserved.

Library of Congress Catalog Card Number 65-25844
ISBN 0-8254-2621-9

This series of sermons selected from
SERMONS ON THE WAY OF SALVATION
by Charles G. Finney.

Reprinted 1975

Printed in the United States of America

PUBLISHER'S FOREWORD

Why this new edition of the sermons of Charles Grandison Finney? Because in many ways the days in which we are living are a duplicate of the day and situation in which Finney himself proclaimed the message which God had given him — the call to evangelism and to revival. These messages speak to our day in no uncertain sound for conditions within the church, and in the world around, call for a voice from God, a resounding clarion call for return to the Biblical standard of Christian life, and the God-ordained plan of redemption and revival.

These have been chosen and arranged with the needs of the world and church today in view. They are as applicable in this day of falling away and departure from the faith as they were in Finney's day. Heart-searching and uncompromising, they cut away the froth and frills so apparent in much modern preaching to reveal God's message for a sinning world, a world seemingly intent upon self-destruction and self-aggrandizement.

It is the publisher's prayer that these messages in their new form will convey God's message to our needy world, revealing His will and purpose for His Church — and His divine plan of salvation for an unbelieving generation.

The Publishers

CONTENTS

1

SALVATION DIFFICULTIES

"If the righteous scarcely be saved, where shall the ungodly and the sinner appear?"— 1 *Peter*. iv. 18

FROM the connection of this passage, some have inferred that the apostle had his eye immediately upon the destruction of Jerusalem. They suppose this great and fearful event to be alluded to in the language, "For the time has come that judgment must begin at the house of God; and if it first begin at us, what shall be the end of them that obey not the gospel of God?" This *may* refer to the destruction of the city and temple of God's ancient people, yet the evidence for the opinion does not seem to be decisive. A reference to the event is possible and even probable. We know that when Jerusalem was destroyed, not one Christian perished. They had timely notice in the signs Christ had already given them, and perceiving those signs in season, they all fled to Pella, on the east of the Jordan, and hence were not involved in the general destruction.

But whether Peter refers to this particular event or not, one thing is plain: he recognises a principle in the government of God, namely, *that the righteous will be saved, though with difficulty, but the wicked will not*

be saved at all. It is plain throughout this whole
chapter that Peter had his mind upon the broad distinction between the righteous and the wicked—a distinction which was strikingly illustrated in the destruction of Jerusalem, and which can never lack illustrations
under the moral and providential government of a holy
God.

The salvation of the righteous, though certain, is
difficult. Though saved, they will be *scarcely* saved.
On this basis rests the argument of the apostle,—that
if their salvation be so difficult, the sinner cannot be
saved at all. His salvation is utterly impossible. This
is plainly the doctrine of the text. It had a striking
exemplification in the destruction of Jerusalem, and
the passage, as I have said, may or may not have reference to that event. All students of the Bible know
that this great destruction is often held up as a type
or model of the final judgment of the world. It was a
great event on the page of Jewish history, and certainly
had great significance as an illustration of God's dealings towards our sinning race.

In pursuing this subject, I purpose to show,

I. WHY THE SALVATION OF THE RIGHTEOUS IS
    DIFFICULT;

II. WHY THE SALVATION OF THE SINNER IS
    IMPOSSIBLE;

III. ANSWER THE QUESTION OF THE TEXT,—
     WHERE SHALL THE UNGODLY AND THE
     SINNER APPEAR?

The difficulty in the salvation of either the righteous or the wicked turns not on any want of mercy in

the heart of God. It is not because God is implacable and hard to be appeased : this is not the reason why the salvation of even the sinner is impossible.

Again, it is not in any lack of provision in the atonement to cover all the wants of sinners, and even to make propitiation for the sins of the world. The Bible nowhere raises the question as to the entire sufficiency of the atonement to do all that an atonement can do or need do for the salvation of our race.

But, positively, one difficulty is found in the nature of God's government, and in the nature of free agency in this world. God has so constituted man as to limit himself to one mode of government over him. This must be moral, and not physical. It must be done by action upon mind *as mind*, and not by such *force* as applies legitimately to move *matter*. If the nature of the case admitted the use of physical force, it would be infinitely easy for God to move and sway such puny creatures as we are. That physical omnipotence which sweeps the heavens and upholds the universe could find no difficulty in moving lumps of clay so small and insignificant as we. But mind cannot be moved as God moves the planets. Physical force can have no direct application to mind for the purpose of determining its moral action. If it should act upon mind as it does upon matter, we certainly know there could be neither moral action nor moral character in such beings as we are. We could not have even a conception of moral conduct. How then could the thing itself possibly exist ?

Men are placed under God's government with such

a created constitution and such established relations to it that they must act freely. God has made them capable of controlling their own moral conduct by the free action of their own wills, and now he expects and requires them to choose between his service and rebellion. Such being the case, the great difficulty is to *persuade sinners to choose right*. God is infinitely ready to forgive them if they will repent ; but the great problem is to persuade them to do so. They are to be prepared for heaven. For this, an entire change of moral character is requisite. This could be done with the utmost ease, if nothing more were needful than to take them into some Jordan stream and wash them, physically, as if from some external pollution, and God should be pleased to employ physical power for this purpose. But the change needed being in its nature *moral*, the means employed must be moral. All the influence must be of a moral character.

Now everybody knows that a moral agent must be able, in the proper sense of this term, to resist every degree of moral influence. Else he cannot be a moral agent. His action must be responsible action, and therefore must be performed of his own free will and accord, no power interposing of such a sort or in such measure as to overbear or interfere with his own responsible agency. Hence the necessity of moral means to convert sinners, to gain their voluntary consent in this great change from sin to holiness, from disobeying to obeying God. And hence the need that this change be wrought, ultimately, by moral means alone.

God may and does employ physical agencies to act morally, but never to act physically. He may send sickness, to reach the heart, but not to purge away any sort of physical sin.

There are a great many difficulties in the way of converting sinners, and saving them when once converted :—many which people are prone to overlook. Hence we must go into some detail, in order to make this matter plain.

One class of these difficulties is the result of an abused constitution. When Adam and Eve were created, their appetites were doubtless mild and moderate. They did not live to please themselves and gratify their own appetites. Their deep and all-engrossing desire and purpose to please God was the law of their entire activities. For a time, therefore, they walked in holy obedience, until temptation came in a particular form, and they sinned. Sin introduced another law—the law of self-indulgence. Every one knows how terribly this law tends to perpetuate and strengthen itself. Every one knows the fearful sway it gains so rapidly over the whole being when once enthroned in power. Now, therefore, the beautiful order and subordination which in holiness obtained throughout all their active powers, was broken up and subverted under the reign of sin. Their appetites lost their proper balance. No longer subordinate to reason and to God, they became inordinate, clamorous, despotic.

Precisely in this does sin consist—in the irrational gratification of the appetites and passions. This is the form in which it appeared in our first parents. Such are its developments in all the race.

Now in order to save men, they must be brought back from this, and restored to a state in which God and reason control the free action of the mind, and appetite is held in due subjection.

Now here let me be understood. The want of balance—the moral disorder of which I speak—is not this, that the will has become enslaved, and has lost its inherent power of free moral action. This is not the difficulty ; but the thing is, that the sensibility has been enormously developed, and the mind accustoms itself to yield to the demands it makes for indulgence.

Here is the difficulty. Some have formed habits and have confirmed them until they have become immensely strong, and it becomes exceedingly difficult to induce them to break away. The rescue must be effected by moral, not by physical means, and the problem is to make the moral means powerful enough for the purpose.

Again, we must notice, among the difficulties in question, the entanglements of a multitude of circumstances. I have often thought it well for Christians that they do not see all their difficulties at first. If they did, its discouraging effect might be disastrous. Coming upon the mind while it is poising the elements of the great question—a life of sin or a life of holiness ; or, after conversion, falling in their power upon the mind while yet its purpose to serve God is but little confirmed, the result might be not only greatly trying, but perhaps fatal. But the ways of God in this, as in all things are admirable. He does not let them see all their future difficulties at first, but lets them come up from time to time in succession, as they have strength to meet them and overcome.

The great difficulty is, living to please self rather than God. It is wonderful to see how much this difficulty is enhanced by the agency Satan and sin have had in the framework of society. It would seem that a bait is held before every man, whatever his position and circumstances may be. One cannot but be astonished at the number of baits provided and laid in the habits and usages, we might perhaps say, in the very construction and constitution, of society. See how men are interlocked in the relations of life,—partners in business, associates in pleasure ; attached in the more endearing and permanent relations of life,—husbands and wives, lovers and loved, parents and children. How many influences of a moral sort, and often tempting to sin, grow out of each, and, Oh, how many out of *all* these complicated and various relations ! Youth of both sexes are educated—perhaps together, perhaps apart ; yet in either case there arises a host of social attractions, and in the history of the race, who does not know that often the resulting influences are evil ? The troubles and cares of business—how often do they " like a wild deluge come," and overwhelm the soul that else would " consider its ways and turn its feet unto God's testimonies " ! How complicated are the sources of irritation that provoke men's spirits to ill-temper, and ensnare them thus into sin ! Many times we marvel and say, What amazing grace is needful

here! What power, less than Almighty, could pluck
God's children from such a network of snares and
toils, and plant them at last on the high ground of established holiness!

There is a man chained to a wife who is a constant
source of temptation and trial to him. There is a wife
who sees scarce a peaceful moment in all her life with
her husband,—all is vexation and sorrow of spirit.

Many parents have children who are a constant trial
to them. They are indolent, or they are reckless, or
they are self-willed and obstinate. Their own tempers
perhaps are chafed, and they become a sore temptation to a similar state of chafed and fretted temper in
their parents. On the other hand, children may have
equal trials in their parents. Where can you find a
family in which the several members are not in some
way a source of trial to each other! Sometimes the
temptation comes in an appeal to their ambition and
pride. Their children have some qualities for the
parents to be proud of, and this becomes a snare to
parents and children both. Oh, how complicated are
the temptations which cross and re-cross every pathway
of human life! Who but God can save against the
power of such temptations?

Many children have been brought up in error. Their
parents have held erroneous opinions, and they have
had their moral constitution saturated with this influence from their cradle and upwards. How terrible
such an influence must inevitably be!

Or, the business of their parents may have been such
as to *mis*educate them—as the business of rum-selling,

for example, and who does not know how terribly this kind of influence cleaves to a man, even as his skin, and seems to become a part of him by pervading the very tissues of his soul!

When the mind gives itself up to self-indulgence, and a host of appetites became clamorous and impetuous, what a labour it must be to bring the soul into harmony with God! How many impulses must be withstood and overcome; how great the change that must be wrought in both the physical and moral state of the man! No wonder that the devil flatters himself that he has got the race of depraved men into his snares and can lead them captive at his will. Think how many thousand years he has been planning and scheming, studying human nature and the laws of depravity, that he may make himself fully master of the hellish art of seducing moral agents away from God and holiness. The truth is, we scarcely begin to realise how artful a devil we have to encounter. We scarcely begin to see how potent an adversary is he who, "like a roaring lion, goes about seeking whom he may devour," and who must be resisted and overcome, or we are not saved.

Many are not aware of the labour necessary to get rid of the influence of a bad education. I speak now of education in the broad comprehensive sense—embracing all that moulds the habits, the temper, the affections, as well as develops the intellect. Ofttimes the affections become unhappily attached, yet the attachment is exceedingly strong, and it shall seem like the sundering of the very heart-strings, to break it off. This

attachment may fasten upon friends, wives, husbands,
or children ; it may make gold its god, and bow down
to such an image. Sometimes we are quite inadequate
to judge of the strength of this attachment, except as
we may see what strange and terrible means God is
compelled to use to sever it. Oh, how does he look
with careful, tearful pity upon his entangled and en-
dangered children, marking the bands that are coiled
around their hearts to bind them to earth, and contriv-
ing how he can best sunder those bands and draw
back their wandering hearts to himself ! We know
he never does afflict willingly, nor grieve the children
of men—never his people but for their profit, that they
may partake of his holiness ; yet who does not know
how often he is compelled to bring tears from their
eyes ; to wring their hearts with many sorrows ; to tear
from them many a fond and loved object of their affections—else he could not save them from their propen-
sities towards sin and self-indulgence ! Oh, what a
work is this which Christ undertakes that he may save
his people from their sins ! How strange and how
complicated are the difficulties ! Who could overcome
them but God !

Again, the darkness of nature is so great and so
gross, that it must be an exceedingly great work to save
them from its influence, and pour the true light of God
through their intelligence. It is by no means sufficient
to know the mere theory of religion, or to know all of
religion that the human mind, unenlightened by the
Divine Spirit, can know. Indeed, Christians never
know themselves except as they see themselves in

God's own light. They need to see God's character in its real nature, and then, in view of what God is, they can see and estimate themselves rightly. This is one important part of the truth on this subject; and another point is, that God himself by his Spirit becomes the teacher of the humble and trustful, and so enlightens the understanding that divine truth can be seen in its real colours and just proportions. And now do you say, O God, show me what I am, and make me know my own heart thoroughly? Did you ever find yourself in doubt and perplexity about your own state, and then, crying for help and light unto God, has he not answered your prayer by first revealing himself and his own character, so that in the light reflected from his character you saw your own, and in the light of his principles of action you saw your own, and in the light shown you as to his heart you also saw your own? You do not see your own state of mind by simply inverting your mental eye and looking within, but by being drawn so near to God that you come into real and deep sympathy with him. Then, seeing and knowing God, you see and know yourself. You cannot help seeing whether your heart responds in sympathy and aim with his, and this very fact reveals your own heart to yourself. It is wonderful how much the Christian learns of himself by truly learning God; and it is not less a matter of wonder and admiration that Christians should experience such moral transformations by simply knowing God, and by being drawn into sympathy with him the more as the more they know him. The great difficulty is that Christians are shy of God—shy—especially as soon as they relapse into the spirit of the world. Then they find an almost resistless inclination to *keep off*, to hold themselves aloof from anything like close communion with God. Hence God is compelled to draw them back, to discipline them with afflictions, to spoil their idols, and dash in pieces their graven images. Always awake and on the alert—so the Bible represents it : " He that keepeth Israel shall never slumber or sleep ". By day and by night he watcheth, and " keepeth them as the apple of his eye ! " How wonderful is such condescension and loving kindness !

Finally, the greatness of the change requisite in passing from sin to real holiness—from Satan's kingdom into full fitness for Christ's, creates no small difficulty in the way of saving even the converted. It is difficult, nay impossible, to make men see this all at once ; and, indeed, if the Christian were to see it all at once, it would not unlikely overwhelm him in despair. Hence God wisely lets him see enough to impress strongly his need of divine aid, and enough to make him cry out, " Who then can be saved ? "

CONCLUSION

But I must make some remarks in application of the subject so far discussed, and reserve the consideration of our remaining points to another time.

We see why the Scriptures are so full of exhortations to Christians to *run*, RUN, and especially to run by *rule*. " He that striveth for the mastery must by all means strive *lawfully*," *i. e.*, according to the rules in such cases made and provided. So let the Christian be careful not only that he runs, but that he runs the right way and in the right manner.

We see, also, why the Christian is exhorted in like manner to fight, grasping the sword, buckling on the shield, putting on the helmet of salvation, preparing himself in all points for a warlike march through an enemy's country, where fighting must be looked for day and night.

Coupled with this is the fitting exhortation to stand fast—to plant his feet firmly and brace himself with all his strength, as if the enemies' hosts were about to charge with the deadly bayonet. Stand fast, their Captain shouteth ; play the man for your king and for yourselves, for the enemy are down upon you in strength and in wrath !

Agonise too, struggle ; for fierce will the conflict be. It is no contemptible foe whom you must face. The Scriptures represent that only the violent take this kingdom of God, and they do it "*by force*". What could be more expressive of the energy to be put forth by Christ's people if they would win the victory and wear the crown ?

We see why Christians are represented as *wrestling*, like men in personal struggle for the mastery. They have a personal enemy to fight and to subdue.

They must, however, give all diligence. A lazy man cannot get to heaven. To get there costs toil and labour. For his will must be sanctified. The entire voluntary department of his being must be renovated. It is remarkable how the Christian warfare develops

the will. Not an obstinate will—not a self-will, do I
mean, but a strong and firm will. The man, disci-
plined in the Christian conflict, cries out, I must and I
will believe ; I will *trust*.

The Christian is also commanded to *watch*—not to
close his eyes for a little more sleep and a little more
slumber. His condition is one of hourly peril, and
therefore, what Christ says to one, he says to *all*—
WATCH. We can see the reason for this in the light
revealed from our subject.

We see, also, why the Christian is to pray always,
as well as to agonise and watch. It is not all to be
done by his own unaided exertions. In fact, one of
his chief exertions should turn upon this very point—
that he pray always, "*watching* thereunto," lest anything draw his heart down from the throne of his Great
Helper.

We may also see why Christians are exhorted to
separate themselves from the world. They are told
they must hang the old man upon the cross. To this
there are no exceptions. Whoever would be saved
must be crucified—that is, as to "the old man and his
deeds". The crucifixion of Christ is an emblem of
this, and serves, therefore, in a measure, to show what
this must and should be.

Does any one suppose that the whole intent of
Christ's crucifixion is to meet the demands of the vio-
lated law ? Not so ; but it was also to be an emblem
of the work to be wrought upon and within the Christian's soul. *Its* old selfish habitudes must be broken
up and its powerful tendencies to evil be slain.

Mark, also, why Christians are exhorted to spend the time of their sojourning here in fear, and to walk softly and carefully, as before God, through all the meanderings of their pilgrimage; in all holy conversation—so reads his book of counsel—being steadfast, immovable, always abounding in work—*the* work, too, of the Lord, as knowing that so his labour will not be in vain in the Lord. Every weight must he lay aside; must not encumber himself with many cares; must not overload himself with gold, nor even with care and effort to get it; must be watchful most diligently on this side and on that, remembering, for both his quickening and his comfort, that Christ, too, with his holy angels, watches evermore over him, saying, I am determined to save you if I can, but I cannot unless I can first gain and then retain your attention, and then rouse up your hearts to the utmost diligence, coupled with the most simple-hearted faith. Oh, what a conflict there must be to rescue each saved sinner from the jaws of Satan and from the thraldom of his own lusts, and finally bring him home, washed and holy, to his home in the heavens! No wonder the Bible should speak of the Christian as being saved only through much difficulty.

Again, sinners, if they will only exercise a little common sense and philosophy, can readily account for the faults of Christians. See that husband with a pious wife. He treats her badly, and day after day annoys her by his ill-temper and little abuses. The children, too, trouble her, and all the more for the example her husband sets before them. Now he may very likely, in some of his moods of mind and temper, drop some reflections upon her piety, and upon the gospel she professes ; but in his more rational moments he will be compelled to say, " No wonder my wife has these faults : I have never helped her at all ; I have only hindered her in all her Christian course, and I know I have been a continual source of vexation and irritation to her. No wonder she has had faults. I am ashamed that I have done so much to create and multiply them, and so very little ever in any way to improve her character."

When candid men come to consider all these things, —the human constitution, the tendency to unbelief, the impulses towards self-indulgence, and the strength of temptation,—they cannot but see that there is abundant occasion for all those faults in Christian character and conduct which they are wont to criticise so stringently. Yet often, perhaps commonly, wicked men make no allowance for the faults of Christians, but assume that every Christian ought to be spotless, while every sinner may make so much apology for his sin as quite to shield his conscience from conviction of guilt. Nothing, therefore, is more common than for impenitent men to triumph, devil-like, over any instance of stumbling in a professed Christian. Why don't they rather sympathise with their difficulties and their great work—as real philanthropists ? That brother who has a Christian sister does not help her at all, but, on the contrary, tries to ensnare her into sin. He should rather say, " I will not be a stumbling block to my sister. If I cannot directly help her on in her Christian course, at least I will not hinder her." Let the impen-itent husband say, "My dear Christian wife! I know something about her difficulties; God forbid that I should play into the devil's hands, and try to help the devil on in his devilish work." Sinner, why don't you abstain from ensnaring your Christian friend? There is One above who cares for him, who patiently toils for his salvation, and watches day and night over his progress, and who is pledged to save him at last. And can you hope to gain the favour of that Holy and Just Being by trying to ensnare and offend any of his little ones?

2

SALVATION OF SINNERS IMPOSSIBLE

"If the righteous scarcely be saved, where shall the ungodly and the sinner appear ? "—1 *Peter* iv. 18.

I SAID in a former sermon, that the doctrine of the text is that the salvation of the righteous is difficult and that of the sinner impossible. In that sermon I discussed at length the first part of this subject, showing how and why the salvation of the righteous is difficult. I am now to take up the remaining part and show how and *why the salvation of the wicked is impossible.*

Here let me premise in general that by the righteous is not meant those who have never sinned. It could not be difficult to save such as had not sinned against God. They are, in fact, already saved. But these righteous ones are those, who, having been sinners, now come to exercise faith in Christ, and of course become " heirs of that righteousness which is by faith ". Vitally important to be considered here is the fact that the governmental difficulty in the way of being saved, growing out of your having sinned, even greatly, is all removed by Christ's atonement. No matter now how great your guilt, if you will only have faith in Jesus, and accept of his atonement as the ground of pardon for your sins.

Hence the difficulty in the way of saving sinners is not simply that they have sinned, but that they will not now cease from sinning and believe on the Lord Jesus Christ.

The salvation of sinners is therefore impossible.

1. Because it is impossible for God by any means he can wisely employ, to persuade them to desist from sinning. They are so wicked and so perverse that they abuse to greater sin the very best means God employs to bring them to repentance. Hence God cannot wisely save them.

When I say it is *impossible* for God to convert them, I do not imply that God lacks *physical* power to do anything which is the proper subject of such power. On this point there can be no question. But how can physical omnipotence be brought to bear directly upon mind and upon the heart ?

Again, let us consider, that it may not be wise for God to bring all the moral power of his universe to bear upon the sinner in this world. If this were wise and practicable, it might avail—for aught we can know ; but since he does not do it, we infer that he refrains for some wise reason.

Certain limitations are fixed in the divine wisdom to the amount of moral influence which God shall employ in the case of a sinner. It is in view of this fact that I say, God finds it impossible to gain the sinner's consent to the gospel by any means that he can wisely employ. He goes as far as is really wise and as far as is on the whole good. This is undoubtedly the fact in the case. Yet all this does not avail. Hence it becomes impossible that the sinner should be saved.

2. Again, the sinner cannot be saved, because salvation *from sin* is an indispensable condition of salvation *from hell*. The being saved from sin must come first in order. Every sinner knows, and on reflection and self-inspection he must see, that his state of mind is such that he cannot respect himself. The elements of blessedness are not therefore in him, and cannot be until he meets the demands of his own moral nature.

He knows, also, that he does not want to have anything to do with God—is afraid of God—both dreads and hates his presence—is afraid to die and go so near to God as death bears all men. He knows that all his relations to God are unpleasant in the extreme. How certainly, then, may he know that he is utterly unprepared for heaven.

Now the sinner must be saved from this guilty and abominable state of mind. No change is needed in God—neither in his character, government, or position towards sin ; but the utmost possible change and all the needed change is requisite on the part of the sinner. If salvation implies fitness for heaven, and if this implies ceasing from sin, then, of course, it is naturally and for ever impossible that any sinner can be saved without holiness.

3. The peace of heaven forbids that you should go there in your sins. I know you think of going to heaven ; you rather expect you shall go there at last ; your parents are there,—as you hope and believe,—

and for this reason you the more want to go, that you may behold them in their glory. Oh, say you, should I not like to be where my father and mother are? And do you think you can follow them, *in your sins?* What could you do in heaven if you were there? What could you say? What kind of songs could you sing there? What sort of happiness, congenial to your heart, could you hope to find there?

Your pious mother in heaven—Oh, how changed! You heard her last words on earth—for they were words of prayer for your poor guilty soul; but now she shines and sings above, all holy and pure. What sympathy could there be between you and her in heaven? Remember what Christ said when some one told him that his mother and his brethren stood without, desiring to see him. "Who," said he, " is my mother? and who are my brethren? He that doeth the will of my Father, the same is my brother, and sister, and mother." The law of sympathy, therefore, in heaven turns not on earthly relationship, but on oneness of heart—on the common and mutual spirit of love and obedience towards their great common Father.

Do you then expect that your mother would be glad to see you—that she would spread her mantle over you and take you up to heaven? Oh, if she were told that you were at the gate, she would hasten down to say, O my sinning child! you cannot enter heaven. Into this holy place nothing can by any means enter that "worketh abomination or maketh a lie". You cannot —no, you cannot come!

If it were left to your own mother to decide the question of your admission, you could not come in. She would not open heaven's gate for your admission. She knows you would disturb the bliss of heaven. She knows you would mar its purity and be an element of discord in its sympathies and in its songs.

You know it need not have been so. You might have given your heart to God in season, and then he would have shed his love abroad in your soul, and given you the Holy Ghost, and made you ripe for heaven. But you *would not*. All was done for you that God could wisely do ; all that Christ could do ; all that the spirit of God could consistently do. But all was vain : all came to naught and availed nothing, because you *would* not forego your sins—would not renounce them, even for everlasting life. And now will heaven let you in ? No. Nothing that worketh abomination can by any means go in there.

4. Besides, it would not be for your own comfort to be there. You were never quite comfortable in spiritual society on earth ; in the prayer-meeting you were unhappy. As one individual said here : " Oh, what a place this is ! I cannot go across the street without being spoken to about my soul. How can I live here ? "

Let me tell you, it will be just as bad, nay, much worse, for you in heaven. That can be no place for you, sinner, since you hate, worst of all things on earth, those places and scenes which are most like heaven.

5. The justice of God will not allow you to partici- pate in the joys of the saints. His relations to the

universe make it indispensable that he should protect
his saints from such society as you. They have had
their discipline of trial in such society long enough :
the scenes of their eternal reward will bring everlasting
relief from this torture of their holy sympathies. Oh,
how will God, their Infinite Father, throw around them
the shield of his protection upon the mountains of paradise, that lift their heads eternally under the sunlight
of his glory !

His sense of propriety forbids that he should give
you a place among his pure and trustful children. It
would be so unfitting—so unsuitable ! It would throw
such discord into the sweet songs and sympathies of
the holy !

Besides, as already hinted, it could be no kindness
to you. It could not soothe, but only chafe and fret
your spirit. Oh, if you were obliged to be there, how
would it torment and irritate your soul !

If, then, the sinner cannot be saved and go to
heaven, *where shall he appear ?*

The question is a strong negation. They shall not
appear among the righteous and the saved. This is a
common form of speaking. Nehemiah said, " Shall
such a man as I *flee ?* " No, indeed. This form of
question is one of the strongest forms of negation that
can be expressed in our language.

Where, then, shall the ungodly and the sinner
appear ? In no desirable place or position—certainly.
Not with the righteous in the judgment, for so God's
word has often and most solemnly affirmed. Christ
himself affirms that, when all nations shall be gathered

before him for judgment, he will separate them, one from another, as a shepherd divideth the sheep from the goats. This separation, as the description shows, brings the righteous on the right hand and the wicked on the left. And it should be considered that this statement is made by Christ himself, and that if any being in the universe knows, it must be he to whom is "given authority to execute judgment". He says he will separate them one from another according not to their national relations, or their family connections, but according to their character as friends or enemies to God.

Oh, what a separation must this be in families and among dear earthly friends! On this side will be a husband—on that a wife; here a brother and there a sister; here one of two friends and there the other—parted for ever—*for ever !* If this great division were to be struck between you to-day according to present character, how fearful the line of separation it would draw! Ask yourselves where it would pass through your own families and among the friends you love. How would it divide College classes—and Oh, how would it smite many hearts with terror and consternation!

It is asked, where shall the ungodly appear? I answer, *certainly not in heaven,* nor on the heavenly side. But they must be in the judgment, for God has said, he would bring all the race into judgment, and every secret thing, whether it be good, or whether it be evil. All are to be there, but some are on the right hand and some on the left.

The ungodly and the sinner will appear in that day among the damned—among lost angels, doomed to the place prepared of old for their eternal abode. So Jesus has himself told us. The very words of their sentence are on record : " Then will he say to them on his left hand, Depart, from me, ye cursed, into ever-lasting fire, prepared for the devil and his angels ". This is indeed the only place for which they are pre-pared ; and this the only society to which their hearts are congenial. They have of choice belonged to Satan's government on earth : at least, in the sense of doing precisely what he would have them do. Now, therefore, after such a training in selfishness and sin, they are manifestly fit for no other and better society than that of Satan and his angels.

Let it not surprise any of you to be told that the amiable sinners of earth are preparing themselves—(re-maining enemies to God and radically selfish)—for the society of the arch spirit of evil. Just observe what restraints are thrown around sinners here. Mark how obviously they *feel* restrained, and show that they are restive and ill at ease. It may be read out of their very hearts that they would be glad to be vastly more wicked and selfish, that is, in their external life—if they might. It is wonderful to see in how many ways God's providence has walled around the sinner's path-way and hedged him in from outbreaking sin.

But let these walls be torn away ; let all regard to his reputation among the good perish for ever from his soul ; let despair of ever gaining God's favour take full possession of his heart, and rivet its iron grasp upon

him, then what will he become? Take away all the restraints of civil society—of laws and customs—of
Christian example, and of Christian society; let there
be no more prayer made for him by pitying Christian
friends, no more counsel given, or entreaty used to
persuade him towards the good, then tell me, where is
the sinner? How terribly will sin work out its dreadful power to corrupt and madden the soul! Bring together myriads of desperate wretches, in the madness
of their despair and rage and wrath against God and
all the good, and Oh what a fearful world would they
make! What can be conceived more awful! Yet this
is the very world for which sinners are now preparing,
and the only one for which they will be found in the
judgment to be prepared.

As this is the only world for which the sinner is prepared, so is it the only one which is appropriate and
fitting, the case being viewed in respect to his influence
for mischief. Here only, here in this prison-house of
woe and despair, can sinners be effectually prevented
from doing any further mischief in God's kingdom.
Here they are cut off from all possibility of doing any
more harm in God's universe.

In this earthly state one sinner destroys much good;
each and every sinner does much evil. God looks on,
not unconcerned, but with amazing patience. He suffers a great deal of evil to be done, for the sake of
securing an opportunity to try the power of forbearance and love upon the sinner's heart. You are abus-
ing his love and defeating all its kind designs, but still
God waits, till the point is reached where forbearance

ceases to be virtue. Beyond this point, how can God wait longer ?

Here you find ample room for doing mischief. Many are around you whom you influence to evil and urge on towards hell. Some of them would be converted but for your influence to hold them back and ensnare their souls. If this were the place, I could name and call out some of you who are exerting a deadly influence upon your associates. Ah, to think of the souls you may ruin for ever! God sees them, and sees how you are playing into the devil's hands to drag them down with you to an eternal hell. But ere long he will take you away from this sphere of doing evil. He will for ever cut off your connection with those who can be influenced to evil, and leave around you only those associates who are ruined, despairing, and maddened in sin, like yourself. There he will lock you up, throw away the key, and let you rave on, and swear on, and curse on, and madden your guilty soul more and more for ever! Oh! what inmates are those in this prison-house of the guilty and the lost! Why should not God fit up *such* a place for *such* beings, so lost to all good, and so given up to all the madness and guilt of rebellion ?

There alone can sinners be made useful. They re-fused to make themselves useful by their voluntary agency on earth; now God will make use of them in hell for some good. Do you ask me if I talk about sin being made useful? Yes, to be sure I do. God never permits anything to occur in his universe but he ex-tracts some good from it, overruling its influence, or making the correction and punishment of it a means of good. This is a great consolation to the holy, that no sinner can exist from whom God will not bring out some good. This principle is partially developed in society here, under civil government. The gallows is not the greatest evil in the world, nor the most unmixed evil. Murder is much worse. States prisons are not the greatest earthly evils. Government can make great use of those men who will not obey law. It can make them examples and lift them up as beacons of warning, to show the evil of disobeying wholesome laws. A great many men have had strong and useful impressions made on their minds, as, riding through Auburn on the railroad, they have marked those lofty frowning walls and battlements which enclose and guard the culprits immured within. Many a hard heart has quailed before those walls, and the terrors of those cells behind. If the outside view does not avail to awe the spirit of transgression, give them the inside view and some of its heart-desolating experience. These things do good. They tame the passion for evil-doing, and impress a salutary fear on the hardened and reckless. If so under all the imperfections of human government, how much more under the perfect administration of the divine!

God cannot afford to lose your influence in his universe. He will rejoice to use you for the glory of his mercy, if you will; Oh yes! He will put away your sins far as the East is from the West, and will put a robe of beauty and glory upon you, and a sweet harp in your hands, and a song of praise on your lips, and the melody of heaven's love in your heart,—all these, if you will. But if you will not, then he has other attributes besides mercy that need to be illustrated. Justice will come in for its claim, and to illustrate this he will make you an example of the bitter misery of sinning. He will put you deep in hell; and the holy, beholding you there, will see that God's kingdom is safe and pure, and in their everlasting song they will shout, "Great and marvellous are thy works, Lord God Almighty; just and true are thy ways, thou King of saints. Who shall not fear thee, O Lord, and glorify thy name? for thy judgments are made manifest."

This is the only way in which God can make you useful in his kingdom, if you will not repent. He has tried every means of bringing you to repentance, but all in vain; he cannot get your consent. Of course there is no alternative but to make you an example to deter all other moral agents from sinning.

There is no other way for God to meet the demands of the public weal, but to make you an example to show his abhorrence of sin. God is most thoroughly economical of his resources. He husbands everything to the very best account. Everything must, under his hand, be made conducive in some way to the general good. Even of your misery he will be as economical as he can, and will carefully turn it all to the very best account. Every groan and every throb and pang of your agonised soul will be turned to use. Yes, rely upon it; all this agony, which does you no good, but is to you only unmingled and unalleviated woe, will be a warning beacon, under God's hand, crying out in

tones of thunder, Stand away! stand away! lest you
come into this place of torment; stand afar from sin—
fear this awful sin—watch against it, for it is an awful
thing to sin against Jehovah. I have tried it and here
I am in woe unutterable! Oh what a testimony, when
all hell shall roll up one mighty accumulated groan! a
groan whose awful voice shall be, Stand in awe and
sin not, for God is terrible in his judgments upon the
guilty.

O sinner, think of it. God wants you now to cry
out to every fellow-sinner, and warn him away from
the brink of hell. Will you do it? What are you in
fact doing? Are you preparing yourself to go out as a
missionary of light and love and mercy to the be-
nighted? Are you pluming your wings, as an angel of
mercy, to bear the messages of salvation? Oh no! you
refuse to do this, or anything of the sort. You disdain
to preach such a gospel and to preach it *so!* But God
will make you preach it *in another way;* for, as I said,
he is thoroughly economical of the resources of his
kingdom, and all must do something in some way for
his glory. He will have everything preach—saints
preach and sinners preach; yea, sinners in hell must
preach for God and for his truth. He will make your
very groans and tears—those "tears that ever fall, but
not in Mercy's sight"—they will preach, and will tell
over and over the dreadful story of mercy abused and
sin persisted in, and waxing worse and worse, till the
bolts of vengeance broke at last upon your guilty head!
Over and over will those groans and tears repeat the
fearful story, so that when the angels shall come from

the remotest regions of the universe, they shall cry out, What is here? What mean those groans? What mean those flames, wreathing around their miserable victims? Ah! the story told then will make them cry aloud, Why will God's creatures sin against his throne? Can there be such madness in beings gifted with reason's light?

These angels know that the only thing that can secure public confidence in a ruler is fidelity in the execution of his law. Hence it is to them no wonder that, there being sin to punish, God should punish it with most exemplary severity. They expect this and seeing its awful demonstrations before their eyes only serves to impress the more deeply on their souls the holiness and justice of the great and blessed God.

CONCLUSION

1. From this standpoint we can easily see what we are to understand by the doctrine of election—a doctrine often misstated, and often perverted to a stone of stumbling and a rock of offence. The simple and plain view of it is, that God, foreseeing all the future of your existence as perfectly as if all were in fact present, determined to deal with you according to your voluntary course; determined to offer you the gospel, and, on your refusal of it, to give you over to the doom of those who deny the Lord that bought them. Election is no new or different plan of divine administration, aside from and unlike what the Bible reveals as the plan of saving men through the gospel. It is this very plan of which the Bible is full, only that it contem-

plates this plan as framed by the divine Mind "before the world began".

2. If you will now consent to give your heart to God, you can be saved. No election will hinder you. The doctrine of election is simply the fact that God sends forth his Spirit to save as many as by the best system of influences he wisely can save; and surely this never can hinder any sinner from repenting and gaining salvation, for the very good reason that this plan contemplates saving and not damning men, as its object, and is in fact the sinner's only hope.

Come then, repent and believe the gospel, if you would be saved. No election will hinder you, and neither will it save you without your own repentance unto life.

How then shall the case turn with you? Almost all who are ever converted are brought in, early in life. Not one in a hundred is converted after the age of forty. The old among the converts are always few— only one among a host—one in a long space of time; like scattering beacon lights upon the mountain tops, that the aged may not quite despair of salvation. But God is intensely interested in saving the young, for he needs and loves to use them in his service. Oh how his heart goes forth after the young! How often has my soul been affected as I have thought of his parental interest for the salvation of this great multitude of youth! They come here from pious homes, freighted with the prayers of pious fathers and mothers,—and what shall be the result? What has been the result, as thus far developed, *with you?* Has anything been really secured as yet? Is anything fixed and done for eternity? How many times have you been called to decide, but have decided wrong—all wrong? You have been pressed earnestly with God's claims, and many a time have prayers and groans gone forth from the Christian heart of this whole community; but ah! where are you still? Not yet safe; ah, in greater peril than ever! Often reproved, hardening your neck; and what next? Suddenly destroyed, and that *without remedy*. Suppose even now the curtain should drop,—*you are dead!* And whither, then, goes the undying, guilty soul?

3. How great the mistake made by Universalists, that all men will be saved, when the Bible holds that even the salvation of the righteous is difficult, and that of the sinner, impossible. How strangely they misread the whole Bible! Go not in their ways, O ye youth of Oberlin!

But what are you doing? Do you flatter yourselves that the work of salvation is all so easy that it may be safely and surely done during a few of life's last moments? Will you presume, as the man did who said he should need but five minutes to prepare to die? Hear his story. What was the result of his system? Disease came on. It smote him with its strong hand. Delirium set in. Reason tottered and fell from her throne, and so he died! Go on, thou young man; drive on, headlong and reckless; make a bold business of sinning, and bear it on with bold front and high hand; but know thou that for all these things God will bring thee into judgment. Consider what tidings we hear of our former pupils who once sat as you now sit, and once heard the gospel as you may hear it now. There, one is dead; and now another—and now another. In rapid succession they drop from the stage of mortal life—and what next? What more? Soon we shall meet them in the fearful judgment!

Brethren, what will the universe say of us, if we neglect to labour for the salvation of these precious youth? What will the parents of these dear youth say to us when we shall meet them at the Saviour's bar?

I have spoken to you of the difficulties and the struggles of the Christian—more and greater far than the ungodly are usually aware of;—those agonies of prayer, those conflicts against temptation; out of all which it is only great grace that can bring him forth, conqueror and more than conqueror. If he is saved with so much difficulty, how does it become you to *strive* to enter in at the strait gate? Are you aware that the smooth sea of temptation bears you on to the breakers of death? Were you ever at Niagara? How smooth and deceitful those waters, as they move along quite up above the draft of the suction from below! But lower down, see how those same waters roar, and dash, and foam, and send up their thick mists to the heavens above you. Yet in the upper stream you glide gently and noiselessly along, dreaming of no danger, and making no effort to escape. In a moment you are in the awful current, dashing headlong down; and where are you now?

And what should you do? Like Bunyan's Christian pilgrim, put your fingers in both ears, and run, shout-

ing, Life! life! eternal LIFE! How many of you are
sliding along on the smooth, deceitful stream, above,
yet only just above, the awful rapids and the dreadful
cataract of death! What if, this night, delirium should
seize upon you? Or what if the Spirit should leave
you for ever, and it should be said of you, " He is joined
to his idols, let him alone"?

What do you say? Do I hear you saying, " If salvation is possible for me—if by putting forth the whole
energy of my will I can ensure it, Oh let me do so!
Help me, O ye ministers of Christ's gospel! Help me,
ye Christians, who pray between the porch and the
altar! Help me, O ye heavens, of heavens for this is
a thing of life and death, and the redemption of the
soul is most precious!"

Surely, O ye sinners, it is time that you should set
down your foot in most fixed determination, and say,
"*I must and I will have heaven!* How can I ever
bear the *doom of the damned!*"

3

THE WRATH OF GOD

"For the wrath of God is revealed from heaven against all ungodliness and unrighteousness of men who hold the truth in unrighteousness."—*Romans* i. 18

THE following context shows that in these words the apostle has his eye especially on those who, not having a written revelation from God, might yet know him in his works of nature. Paul's view is that God's invisible attributes become apparent to the human mind, ever since the creation of our world—being revealed by the things he has made. In and by means of these works, we may learn his eternal power and his real divinity. Hence all men have some means of knowing the great truths that pertain to God, our infinite Creator. And hence God may, with the utmost propriety, hold men responsible for accepting this truth reverently, and rendering to their Creator the homage due. For withholding this, they are utterly without excuse.

I. In discussing the subject presented in our text, let us inquire, first, *What is the true idea of unrighteousness?*

Beyond question, it cannot be less than the negation of righteousness, and may imply more or less of positive wickedness. Here the question will arise, *What is righteousness?* To which I answer, rightness—*moral* rightness, the original term being used in regard to material things, to denote what is straight; as, for example, a straight line. Unrighteousness, the opposite of this, must mean what is morally crooked, distorted—not in harmony with the rightness of God's law. To denote *sin*, the Scriptures employ some terms which properly signify a negation, or utter absence of what should be. Some theologians have maintained that the true idea of sin is simply *negative*, supposing sin to consist in *not* doing and *not* being what one ought to do and to be. This idea is strongly implied in our text. Sin is, indeed, a neglect to do known duty and a refusal to comply with known obligation. Inasmuch as love is required always and of all men, this must be a state of real disobedience. Suffice it, then, to say, that unrighteousness is an omission—a known omission—a refusal to *be* what we should, and to *do* what we should. Of course it is only and wholly voluntary. The mind's refusal to obey God is a matter of its own free choice.

II. What is implied in "holding the truth in unrighteousness"?

The meaning of the original term "hold" is to hold back, to restrain. The idea here is that the man restrains the legitimate influence of the truth, and will not let it have its proper sway over his will.

The human mind is so constituted that truth is its natural stimulus. This stimulus of truth would, if not restrained and held back, lead the mind naturally to obey God. The man holds back the truth through his own unrighteousness, when, for selfish reasons, he over-rules and restrains its natural influence, and will not suffer it to take possession and hold sway over his mind.

III. What is intended by " the wrath of God revealed from heaven" ? and *Why is it thus revealed against all such unrighteousness ?* The obvious sense is that God, manifesting himself from heaven, has revealed his high and just displeasure against all restraining of the truth and withstanding of its influence.

Before I proceed to show why this is, I must be permitted to come very near to some of you whom I see before me this day, and talk to you in great frankness and faithfulness. I do not charge on you that you have been outwardly immoral, but you *have restrained the truth*, you have withstood its influence. You are therefore the very persons against whom the wrath of God it said to be revealed. This is true of every one of you who has not given himself up to the influence of truth. You have restrained that natural influence ; therefore, against *you* God has revealed his wrath.

This is a terrible thing. The wrath of a king is terrible ; how much more so is the wrath of *God !* Ah, who can stand before him when once he shall arise in his wrath to avenge his truth and his own glorious name !

Why does God's wrath wax hot against this sin ? Comprehensively, the reason is this, Withstanding the truth is resisting God's revealed claims of love and obedience, and is therefore the *whole of sin.* All is comprised in it. This is the very essence—the true idea of sin ; it is *deliberate, intelligent, and intentional rebellion against God.* There could be no obligation until your conscience affirms it to yourself. The conscience cannot thus affirm obligation until there is some knowledge of God revealed to the mind ; but when this knowledge is revealed, then conscience must and will affirm obligation. Subsequently to this point, the more conscience is developed, the more it unfolds, and the more strongly it affirms your obligation to obey God. Suppose a person were created asleep. Until he awakes, there could be in his mind no knowledge of God—not one idea of God, and consequently no sense of obligation to obey him. But as soon as the moral functions of the reason and the conscience create a sense of obligation, then the mind is brought to a decision. It must then either choose to obey or to disobey God. It must elect either to take God's law as its rule of duty or to reject it.

The alternative of rejecting God makes it necessary to hold back the truth and withstand its claims. We might almost say that these processes are substantially identical—resisting the natural influence of God's truth on the mind, and withstanding the known claims of God. When you know the truth concerning God, the great question being whether or not you will obey it, if your heart says No ! you do of course resist the claims of truth :—you hold it back through your own unrighteousness.

The very apprehending of moral truth concerning

God renders it impossible to be indifferent. Once seeing God's claims you cannot avoid acting upon them
one way or the other. Hence to stop there after your
duty is made known, and hold your minds aloof from
obedience, is being just as wicked as you can be. You
disown your whole obligation towards God, and practically say unto him, "Depart from me, for I desire not
the knowledge of thy ways". Is not this as wicked as
you can be, with the light you may have at the time?
What more wicked thing could you do?

Let us look at this matter a little farther. Holding
back the truth through unrighteousness implies the to-
tal rejection of the moral law as a rule of duty. This
must be the case, because, when light concerning the
meaning of this law comes before the man, he repels it
and resists its claims, thus virtually saying, That law is
no rule of duty to me. Thus resisting the influence of
truth, he practially denies all obligations to God.
Truth coming before his mind, he perceives his obligation, but he withholds his mind from its sway.

You may probably have observed that some persons
seem to have no sense of any other obligation save that
created by human law. Legal obligation can reach
them, but not moral. They will not pay an honest
debt unless it is in such a shape that the strong hand of
the law can take hold of them. Others have no sensibility to any claims save those that minister to their
business reputation. Take away their fear of losing
this; remove all the inducements to do right, save those
that pertain to moral obligation, and see if they will
ever do anything.

Now such men practically reject and deny God's
rights altogether, and, equally so, their own obligations
to God. Their conduct, put into words, would read, I
have some respect for human law and some fear of
human penalty ; but, for God's law or penalty either,
I care nothing !

It is easy to see that to hold back the truth thus is
the perfection of wickedness. For suppose a man refrains from sinning, only because of his obligations
to human laws. Then he shows that he fears human
penalties only, and has no fear of God before his
eyes.

Again, this holding the truth in unrighteousness settles all questions as to the moral character. You may
know the man with unerring certainty. His position
is taken; his course is fixed ; as to moral obligation, he
cares nothing. The fact perceived, moral obligation
does not decide his course at all. He becomes totally
dishonest. This settles the question of his character.
Until he reveres God's authority, there is not a particle of moral goodness in him. He does not act with
even common honesty. Of course his moral character
towards God is formed and is easily known. If he had
any moral honesty, the perceived fact of his own moral
obligation would influence his mind. But we see it
does not at all ; he shuts down the gate on all the
claims of truth, and will not allow them to sway his
will. Hence it must be that his heart is fully com-
mitted to wickedness.

The wrath of God is revealed from heaven against
all who thus hold back the truth, because this attitude

of the will shows that you are reckless of your obligations towards God. It shows that, with you, a moral
claim on your heart and conscience goes for nothing.
If you restrain the truth from influencing your mind,
this very fact proves that *you do not mean to serve God*.
Some of you know that you are not doing what you see
to be your duty. You are conscious that the presence
of known duty does not move you. You have not
done one act of obedience to God's claims because they
are God's.

Again, not only does this settle the question of moral
character—which is of itself a good reason for God's
wrath;—but it also settles the question of *moral relations*. Because it shows that your moral character is
altogether corrupt and wrong, it also shows that, in regard to moral relations, you are really God's enemy.
From that moment when you resist the claims of moral
truth, God must regard you as his enemy, and not by
any means as his obedient subject. Not in any figurative sense, but in its most literal sense, *you are his
enemy*, and therefore he must be highly displeased with
you. If he were not, his own conscience would condemn him. You must know that it must be his duty
to reveal to you this displeasure. Since he must feel
it, he ought to be open and honest with you. You
could not, in reason, wish him to he otherwise. All
of you who know moral truth, yet obey it not; who
admit obligation which yet you refuse to obey, you are
the men who hold the truth in unrighteousness. Let
this be settled in every one of your minds, that if you
restrain the influence of any truth known concerning

God and your duty, then *against you* is his wrath revealed from heaven.

IV. We must next inquire, *Wherein and how is this wrath revealed ?*

Perhaps some of you are already making this inquiry. Moralists are wont to make it, and to say, "We do not see any wrath coming. If we are as good as professors of religion, why shall we not be saved as well as they?"

Wherein then is God's wrath revealed against this great wickedness.

1. Your conscience affirms that God must be displeased with you. It certifies to you beforehand that you are guilty, and that God cannot accept you.

2. The remorse which will sometimes visit such sinners yet more confirms God's displeasure. True, the feeling of remorse belongs to the sensibility ; but none the less does it give admonitory warning. Its voice must be accounted as the voice of God in the human soul. He who made that sensibility so that it will sometimes recoil under a sense of guilt, and turn back to consume the life and joy of the soul, did not make it a *lie*. It is strange that any should suppose this remorse to be itself the punishment threatened of God against sin, and the whole of it. Far from it. This is not that punishment which God has threatened ; it is only a premonition of it.

The very fears men feel are often to be taken as an indication that the thing they dread is a reality. Why is it that men in their sins are so often greatly afraid to die? It is no other than a trumpet-tone of the voice of God, sounding up from the depths of their very nature. How can they overlook the fact that these grim forebodings of coming doom are indeed a revelation of wrath, made in the very nature God has given them!

Another revelation of God's wrath he makes in his juridical abandonment of sinners. God manifests his despair of doing anything more for their salvation when he manifestly withdraws his Spirit and gives them over to hopeless abandonment. Withdrawing his Spirit, he leaves them in great moral blindness. They may have been able to see and to discriminate spiritual things somewhat before, but, after God forsakes them, they seem almost utterly void of this power. Everything is dark; all is confused. The light of the Holy Spirit being withdrawn, it were practically vain for the sinner himself, or for his sympathising friends, to expect his salvation. This mental darkness over all spiritual things is God's curse on his rejection of truth, and significantly forebodes his speedy doom.

Analogous to this is the indication given in a moral paralysis of the conscience. Strangely it seems to have lost its sensibility; its ready tact in moral discrimination is gone; its perceptions seem unaccountably obtuse, and the tone of its voice waxes feeble and almost inaudible. Practically, one might almost as well have no conscience at all.

What does this paralysis of conscience indicate? Plainly, that God has abandoned that soul. The conscience, so long overborne by a perverse will, gives way, and God ceases longer to sustain its vitality.

It is painful to see how persons in this condition

strain their endeavours, but such debility comes down
upon them—they become so indifferent; diverting influences are so potent—they drop their endeavours, pow-
erless.   Once their conscience had some activity; truth
fell on their mind with appreciable force, and they were
aware of resisting it; but, by-and-by, there ensued a
state of moral feeling in which the mind is no longer
conscious of refusing;—indeed, it seems scarcely conscious of anything whatever.   He has restrained the influence of truth until conscience has mainly suspended
its functions.   Like the drunkard, who has lost all per-
ception of the moral wrong of intemperance, and who
has brought this insensibility on himself by incessant
violations of his better judgment, so the sinner has re-
fused to hear the truth, until the truth now refuses to
move him.   What is the meaning of this strange phe-
nomenon?   It is one of the ways in which God reveals
his indignation at man's great wickedness.

An ungodly student, put on the intellectual race-
course alongside of his class-mates, soon becomes ambitious and jealous.   At first, he will probably have
some sense of this sin; but he soon loses this sense,
and passes on as if unconscious of any sin.   What is
this but a revelation of God's displeasure?

Again, this wrath against those who hold back
the truth in unrighteousness is abundantly revealed in
God's word.   Think of what Christ said to the hypo-
critical scribes and Pharisees, "Fill ye up, then, the
measure of your fathers".   What did he mean by that?
Their fathers had filled their cup of sin till God could
bear with them no longer, and then he filled up his cup

of wrath and poured it forth on the nation, and "*there was no remedy*". So Christ intimates it shall be with the scribes and Pharisees. And what is this but to reveal his wrath against them for holding back the truth through unrighteousness?

Again, he lets such sinners *die in their sins*. Observe how, step by step, God gave them one revelation after another of his wrath against their sin ;—remorse, moral blindness, decay of moral sensibility, and the plain assertions of his word. All these failing, he gives them up to some strong delusion, that they may believe a lie. God himself says, "For this cause God shall send them strong delusion, that they should believe a lie, that they all might be damned who believed not the truth, but had pleasure in unrighteousness". It is painfully instructive to study the workings of modern delusions, especially spiritualism ; to notice how it has come in following the track of those great revivals that blessed our country a few years since. Do not I know scores of persons who passed through those revivals unblessed, and now they are mad with this delusion? They saw the glory of God in those scenes of revival power ; but they turned away, and now they are mad on their idols, and crazy under their delusions. God has given them up to die in their sins, and it will be *an awful death !* Draw near them gently, and ask a few kind questions ; you will soon see that they make no just moral discriminations. All is dark which needs to be light, ere they can find the gate of life.

CONCLUSION

1. You may notice the exact difference between saints and sinners, including among sinners all professors of religion who are not in an obedient state of mind. The exact difference is this, saints have adopted God's will as their law of activity, the rule that shall govern all their life and all their heart. You reveal to them God's will; this settles all further controversy. The very opposite of this is true of the sinner. With him, the fact of God's supposed will has no such influence at all; usually no influence of any sort, unless it be to excite his opposition. Again, the Christian, instead of restraining the influence of truth, acts up to his convictions. If the question of *oughtness* is settled, all is settled. Suppose I go to Deacon A. or Deacon B. and I say, " I want you to do a certain thing; I think you must give so much of your money to this object ". He replies, " I don't know about that, my money costs me great labour and pains ". But I resume, and say, " Let us look calmly at this question " ; and then I proceed to show him that the thing I ask of him is, beyond a doubt, his *duty* to God and to man. He interposes at once, " You need not say another word; that is enough. If it is my duty to Christ and to his people, I ask no more." But the sinner is not moved so. He knows his duty beforehand, but he has long been regardless of its claims on him. You must appeal to his selfish interests, if you would reach his heart. With the Christian, you need not appeal to his hopes or his fears. You only need show his duty to God. The

sinner you can hope to move only by appeals to his
interests.   The reason of this is that his adopted course
of life is to serve his own interests, nothing higher.

2. With sinners the question of religion is one of loss
and gain.   But with Christians, it is only a question of
right and duty towards God.   This makes truth to him
all important, and duty imperative.   But the sinner
only asks, What shall I gain? or What shall I lose?
It is wholly a question of danger.   Indeed, so true is
this, that ministers often assume that the only availing
motive with a sinner must be an appeal to his hopes
and fears.   They have mostly dropped out the consideration of *right* as between the sinner and God.   They
seem to have forgotten that so far forth as they stop
short of the idea of right, and appeal only to the sinner's selfishness, their influence tends to make *spurious
converts*.   For if men enter upon the Christian life only
for *gain* in the line of their hopes and fears, you must
keep up the influence of these considerations, and must
expect to work upon these only ; that is, you must expect to have selfish Christians and a selfish church.   If
you say to them, " This is duty," they will reply,
" What have we ever cared for *duty ?* We were never
converted to the doctrine of doing our duty.   We
became Christians at all, only for the sake of promoting
our own interests, and we have nothing to do in the
Christian life on any other motive."

Now observe, they may modify this language a little
if it seem too repugnant to the general convictions of
decent people ; but none the less is this their real
meaning.   They modify its language only on the same

general principle of making everything subservient to self.

3. Again, we see how great a mistake is made by those selfish Christians who say, " Am I not honest towards my fellow-men? And is not this a proof of piety?"

What do you mean by "honest"? Are you really honest towards God? Do you regard God's rights as much as you wish him to regard yours? But perhaps you ask as many do, What is my crime? I answer, Is it not enough for you to do nothing, really *nothing*, towards obedience to God? Is it not something serious that you refuse to do God's will and hold back the claims of his truth? What's the use of talking about your *morality*, while you disregard the greatest of all moral claims and obligations—those that bind you to love and obey God? What can it avail you to say perpetually, Am I not moral and decent towards men?

Why is God not satisfied with this?

4. Ye who think you are almost as good as Christians;—in fact, it is much nearer the truth to say that you are almost as bad as devils! Indeed you are fully as bad, save that you do not know as much, and therefore cannot be so wicked. You say, " We are kind to each other ". So are devils. Their common purpose to war against God compels them to act in concert. They went in concert into the man possessed with a legion of devils, as we learn in the gospel history. Very likely they are as kind toward each other, in their league against God and goodness, as you are towards

your neighbours. So that selfish men have small ground
to compliment themselves on being kind and good to
each other, while they withstand God, since, in both
these respects, they are only like devils in hell.

5. And now, my impenitent hearers—what do you
say? Putting your conduct towards God into plain language, it would run thus: "Thou, Lord, callest on me
to repent; I shall refuse. Thou dost strive to enforce
my obligation to repent by various truths; I hold back
those truths from their legitimate influence on my mind.
Thou dost insist on my submission to thy authority;
I shall do no such thing."

This, you will see, is only translating your current
life and bearing towards God, into plain words. If you
were really to lift your face toward heaven and utter
these words, it would be blasphemy. What do you
think of it *now?* Do you not admit, and often assert,
that actions speak louder than words? Do they not
also speak more *truthfully?*

6. To those of you who are business men, let me
make this appeal. What would you think of men who
should treat you as you treat God? You take your
account to your customer and you say to him, This account, sir, has been lying a long time past due; will
you be so good as to settle it? You cannot deny that
it is a fair account of value received, and I understand
you have abundant means to pay it. He very coldly
refuses. You suggest the propriety of his giving some
reasons for this refusal; and he tells you it is a fine
time to get large interest on his money, and he therefore finds it more profitable to loan it out than to pay

his debts. That is all. He is only selfish; all there is of it is simply this, that he cares for his own interests supremely, and cares little or nothing for yours when the two classes of interests—his and yours—come into competition.

When you shall treat God as well as you want your creditors to treat you, then you may hold up your head as, so far, an honest man; but, so long as you do the very thing towards God which you condemn as infinitely mean from your fellow-men towards yourself, you have little ground for self-complacent pride.

All this would be true and forcible, even if God were no greater, no better, and had no higher and no more sacred rights than your own. How much more, then, are they weighty beyond expression, since God is so much greater, better, and holier than mortals!

4

SO GREAT SALVATION

" How shall we escape if we neglect so great salvation ? "—*Hebrews*
ii. 3

ESCAPE *what ?* What can Universalists say to such
a question as this? They whose first doctrine pro-
claims that there can be no danger—what will they
say to this solemn question and its startling assumption of peril from which there shall be no escape?
How shall we escape? says the inspired author; as
if he would imply most strongly that there can be no
escape to those who neglect this great salvation.

Salvation ;—the very term imports safety or deliverance from great impending evil. If there be no such
evil, there is no meaning to this term—no real salvation.

The writer is speaking of the salvation published in
the gospel; and the idea that immediately suggested
its greatness is the greatness of its author and revealer.
It is because Jesus Christ, by whom this gospel came,
is so great, compared with angels, that the writer con-
ceives of this salvation as pre-eminently great and glorious.

This second chapter is closely connected with the

first. The train of thought reverts to the fact that God had anciently spoken to their fathers by the prophets ; but in these last days, by his Son—the very brightness of his own glory—the Upholder of all things, shown all through the Bible to be higher than angels, through whose ministrations, also, the divine word had sometimes come to mortals. Now, then, since the word, so revealed by angels, carried with it the sternest authority ; and every sort of transgression and disobedience received a just recompense of reward, how shall men escape who neglect a salvation so great that even God's glorious Son is sent from heaven to earth to reveal it ! He, the *Exalted Son*, come down to create and reveal this salvation ; he wrought it out in death, confirming his divine mission while he lived, by miracles ; must it not then be a matter of supreme importance ?

Yet the Bible has not left us to infer its greatness from the glory of its Author alone ; it presents to us the greatness of this salvation in many other points of view.

It is great in its very *nature*. It is *salvation from death in sin*.

Let men talk and gainsay as they will, this one great fact is given us by human consciousness, *that men are dead in sin*. Every man knows this. We all know that, apart from God's quickening Spirit, we have no heart to love God. Each sinner knows that, whatever may be his powers as a moral agent, yet, left to himself, there is in him a moral weakness that effectually shuts him off from salvation, save as God interposes with efficient help. Hence the salvation that meets him in this weakness, and turns him effectually to love and to please God, must be intrinsically great.

Again, it is great because it *delivers from endless sinning and suffering*.

Just think of that:—*endless suffering*. How long could you bear even the slightest degree of pain, supposing it to continue without intermission? How long ere you would find it unendurable? Experiments in this matter often surprise us; such, for example, as the incessant fall of single drops of water upon the head, —a kind of torture sometimes inflicted on slaves. The first drops are scarcely noticed; but, ere long, the pain becomes excruciating, and ultimately unendurable.

Just think of any kind of suffering which goes on ever increasing! Suppose it to increase constantly for one year; would you not think this to be awful? Suppose it to increase without remission for one hundred years; can you estimate the fearful amount? What, then, must it be if it goes on increasing *for ever!*

It matters not how rapid or how slow this increase; the amount, if its duration be eternal, must be ineffably appalling! Nor does it matter much how great or how little the degree at the outset; suppose it ever so small, yet eternal growth must make it beyond measure appalling! You may suppose the amount of woe endured to be represented by one drop for the first thousand years; yet let it increase for the next thousand, and yet more for the next, and, ere eternity shall have rolled away, the amount will be an *ocean!* It would take a great while to fill up such an ocean as the Atlantic by giving it one drop in each thousand years—yet time would fill it; it would take yet longer to fill the Pacific at the same rate—but time would suffice to fill it; more time would fill up the Indian Ocean; more yet would cover this globe; more would fill all the vast space between us and fixed stars; but even this lapse of time would not exhaust eternity. It would not even begin to measure eternal duration. How fearful, then, must be that woe which knows no limit save eternity!

Some deny the sufferings of the wicked to be penal inflictions, and insist that they are only the natural consequence of sinning. I shall not stop now to enter upon any argument on this point; but I ask, What difference does that make as to the amount or endurableness of eternal woe? Penal or not penal, the Bible represents it as eternal, and its very nature shows that it must be for ever increasing. How, then, can it be essentially lessened by the question, whether it be or be not penal infliction? Whether God has so constituted all moral agents that their sin, allowed to work out its legitimate results, will entail misery enough to answer all those fearful descriptions given us in the Bible, or whether, in addition to all that misery, God inflicts yet more, penally, and this enlarged amount makes up the eternal doom denounced on the finally wicked, it surely can be of small consequence to decide,—so far forth as *amount* of suffering is concerned.

Some deny that the cause of this suffering is material fire. They may even scoff at this and think that, by so doing, they have extinguished the flames of hell, and have thus annihilated all future punishment. How vain! Can a sinner's scoff frustrate the Almighty? Did the Almighty God ever lack means to execute his word? What matters it, whether the immediate agent in the sinner's sufferings be fire or something else of which fire is the fittest emblem? Can your scoffs make it any the less fearful?

This fearful woe is the fruit of sinning; and is therefore inevitable, save as you desist from sinning while yet mercy may be found. Once in hell, you will know that, while you continue to sin, you must continue to suffer.

The language used in the Bible to describe the sinner's future woe is very terrible. We may call it figurative. I suppose those terms to be figures of speech, but I cannot tell. I have never been there. If any one here has been, let him speak.

It certainly *may* be literal fire. No one of us can certainly know that it is not. It must be something *equal to* fire; for we cannot suppose that God would deceive us. Whoever else may speak extravagantly, God never does! He never puts forth great swelling words of vanity—sounding much, but meaning little. Take it, then, which way you please, it is an awful revelation—to die in your sins; to go away into a furnace of fire; to be among those the smoke of whose torment ascendeth up for ever and ever! How strikingly is this doom symbolised in the smoke of those doomed cities of the plain, " set forth as an example, suffering the vengeance of eternal fire"! Their "smoke ascended as the smoke of a great furnace". Abraham lifted up his eyes and saw it! What sort of a night did he spend after that appalling scene? He had risen early, had made his way through the morning dew to the hill-top overlooking Sodom, and then he saw the smoke of those doomed cities ascending to heaven. So may the Christian parent perhaps wend his way to the hill-tops of the heavenly city, and look over into the great pit, where the ungodly weep and wail for evermore! Shall it be that any of your unsaved children will be deep in that pit of woe!

Observe again, this salvation is not merely *negative*—a salvation from sin and from suffering; it has also a *positive* side. On this positive side, it includes perfect holiness and endless blessedness. It is not only deliverance from never-ending and ever-accumulating woe; it is also endless bliss—exceeding, in both kind and degree, all we can conceive in this life. This is not the world to realise the full bliss of unalloyed purity. There will be sin around us; there will yet be some sad traces of it within us. Yet who of us does not sometimes catch a distinct view of that purity and blessedness which we know reigns in heaven? Most blessed views these are, yet no doubt dim and weak, compared with the great reality. When that bliss shall be perfect; when nothing more is left us to desire, but every desire of our soul is filled to its utmost capacity, and we shall have the full assurance that this blessedness must increase with the expansion of our powers and with our advance in knowledge as we gaze with ever-growing interest into the works of the great God, this will be *heaven!* All this is only one side—the positive side of that blessedness which comes with this great salvation.

Now set yourselves to balance these two things, one against the other; an ever-growing misery and an ever-growing blessedness. Find some measuring line by which you can compare them.

You may recall the figure I have more than once mentioned here. An old writer says, Suppose a little bird is set to remove this globe by taking from it one grain of sand at a time, and to come only once in a thousand years. She takes her first grain, and away she flies on her long and weary course, and long, long, are the days ere she returns again. It will doubtless seem to many as if she never would return ; but when a thousand years have rolled away, she comes panting back for one more grain of sand—and this globe is again lessened by just one grain of its almost countless sands. So the work goes on. So eternity wears away —only it does not exhaust itself a particle. That little bird will one day have finished her task, and the last sand will have been taken away ; but even then eternity will have only begun : its sands are never to be exhausted. One would suppose that the angels would become so old, so hoary, with the weight of centuries, and every being so old, they would be weary of life ; but this supposing only shows that we are judging of the effects of time in that eternal state by its observed effect in this transient world. But we fail to consider that God made this world for a transient life—*that* for one that shall never pass away.

Taking up again our figure of the little bird removing the sands of our globe, we may extend it, and suppose that, after she had finished this world, she takes up successively the other planets of our system—Mercury, and Venus, Mars, Jupiter, Saturn, and Herschel, each and all on the same law—one grain each thousand years, and when these are all exhausted, then the sun, and then each of the fixed stars ; until the hundreds of thousands of those stupendous orbs are all removed and gone. But even then eternity is not exhausted. We have not yet even an approximation towards its end. End? There is no end! That poor old bird makes progress. Though exceedingly slow, she will one day have done her appointed task. But she will not even then have come any nearer to the end of eternity! Eternity! Who can compute it? No finite mind ; and yet this idea is not fiction, but sober fact. There is no possible room for mistake—no ground for doubt.

Moreover, no truth can be more entirely and intensely practical than this. Every one of us here—every one of all our families, every child—all these students—are included. It concerns us all. Before us, each and all, lies this eternal state of our being. We are all to live in this eternal state. There awaits us there either woe or bliss, without measure and beyond all our powers of computation. If woe, it will be greater than all finite minds can conceive. Suppose all the minds ever created were to devote their powers to compute this suffering—to find some adequate measure that shall duly represent it ;—alas, they could not even begin! Neither could they any better find measures to contain the *bliss*, on the other hand, of those who are truly the children of God. All the most expressive language of our race would say, It is not in me to measure infinite bliss or infinite woe; all the figures within the grasp of all created imaginations would fade away before the stupendous undertaking; Yet this infinite bliss and endless woe are the plain teaching of the Bible, and are in harmony with the decisive affirmations of the human reason. We know that, if we continue in sin, the misery must come upon us;—if we live and die in holiness, the bliss will come.

And is this the theme, and are these the great facts, which these young men may go abroad to the ends of the world and proclaim to every creature, and which these young women also may speak of everywhere in the society where they move? Truly they have a glorious and sublime message to bear!

Again, suppose the joy resulting from this salvation to be a mild form of peace and quiet of soul. We may suppose this, although we cannot forget that the Bible represents it as being a "joy unspeakable and full of glory"; but suppose it were only a mild, quiet joy. Even then, an eternal accumulation of it—a prolongation of it during eternal ages, considering, also, that naturally it must for ever increase—will amount to an infinite joy. Indeed, it matters little how small the unit with which you start, yet let there be given an eternal duration, coupled with ceaseless growth and increase, and how vast the amount!

According to the Bible, this blessedness of the holy

is the full fruition of God's love. Hence the bliss which it involves can be nothing short of infinite. It can have no limit. A really comprehensive view of what it will be would be overpowering. Who of you could bear the view of your future selves? Could you who are saints? Suppose you could see yourselves as you will exist ten thousand years hence. Suppose you were for a moment endowed with the power to penetrate the future and see yourself as you will be before the throne of God. If you were not apprised that it is yourself, you might fall down and worship!

Or suppose the wicked could see their future selves as they will be ten thousand years hence; could see how full of torment they will be, and what unutterable woes their souls shall bear there,—could they endure the sight?

And here does some one say, How very extravagant you are! Extravagant? Nothing can be further from the truth than to hold these views to be extravagant. For, grant only *immortality*, and all that I have said must follow of necessity. Let it be admitted that the soul exists for ever, and not a word that I have said is too much. Indeed, when you carry out that great fact to its legitimate results under the moral government of God, all these descriptions seem exceedingly flat—they fall so very far short of the truth.

In the next place, let it be considered that neglect of this great salvation is fatal. So our text most emphatically implies, so the Bible often elsewhere most unqualifiedly affirms. No sinner, therefore, need go about to weary himself to commit iniquity, as if he would fain make sure his doom ; for mere neglect is fatal. What more should he want ?

But let us inquire, What is to be regarded as *fatal* neglect? For all have, at some time, been guilty of some neglect.

We shall reach the true answer to our question by asking another, *viz.* What is *effectual attention ?*

Plainly that, and only that, which ensures gospel repentance and faith in Christ ; only that which ensures personal holiness and, thus, final salvation. That is, therefore, effectual attention which arouses the soul thoroughly to take hold of Jesus Christ as the offered Saviour. To fall short of this is fatal neglect. You may have many good things about you—may make many good resolves and hopeful efforts ; yet, failing in this main thing, you fail utterly.

CONCLUSION

1. You need only be a little less than fully in earnest, and you will certainly fall short of salvation. You may have a good deal of feeling and a hopeful *earnestness ;* but if you are only less than fully in earnest, you will surely fail. The work will not be done. You are guilty of fatal neglect, for you have never taken the decisive step. Who of you is he that is a little less than fully in earnest ? You are the one who will weary yourself for naught and in vain. You must certainly fall short of salvation.

2. It must be great folly to do anything short of effectual effort. Many are just enough in earnest to deceive themselves. They pay just enough attention

to this subject to get hold of it wrong, and do only just enough to fall short of salvation, and go down to death with a lie in their right hand. If they were to stay away from all worship, it would shock them. Now, they go to the assemblies of God's people and do many things hopeful; but, after all, they fall short of entering in at the door into Christ's fold. What folly is this! Why should any of you do this foolish thing! This doing only just enough to deceive yourself and others, is the very course to please Satan. Nothing else could so completely serve his ends. He knows very well that where the gospel is generally understood, he must not preach infidelity openly, nor Universalism, nor atheism. Neither would do. But if he can just keep you along, doing a little less than enough, he is sure of his man. He wants to see you holding fast to a false hope. Then he knows you are the greatest possible stumbling-block, and are doing the utmost you can to ruin the souls of men.

3. This salvation is life's great work. If not made such, it had best be left alone. To put it in any other relation is worse than nothing. If you make it second to anything else, your course will surely be ineffectual —a lie, a delusion, a damnation!

Are you giving your attention effectually to this great subject? *Who* of you are? Have you this testimony in your own conscience, that you seek first the kingdom of God and his righteousness? And have you become acquainted with Christ? Do you know him as your Life and your Hope? Have you the joy and peace of believing? Can you give to yourself and to

others a really satisfactory reason for the hope that is
in you ?

This is life's great work—the great work of earth;
and now, in whom of you is it effectually begun? You
cannot do it at all without a thorough and right beginning. I am jealous of some of you that you have not
begun right—that you have mistaken conviction for
conversion. Like some of Bunyan's characters, I fear
you have clambered over the wall into the palace, and
did not come in by the gate. Do you ask me why I
fear this of you ? I will answer only by asking a question back. Don't you think I have reason to fear it?
Have you the consciousness of being pure in heart, and
of growing purer? Do you plan everything with reference to this great work of salvation ? What are the
ways of life that you have marked out for yourself?
and on what principle have you shaped them? On
what subjects are you most sensitive ? What most
thoroughly awakens your sensibility? If there is a
prayer-meeting to pray for the salvation of sinners, are
you there ? Is your heart there?

4. It is infinite folly to make the matter of personal
salvation only a secondary matter; for to do so is only
to neglect it after all. Unless it has your whole heart,
you virtually neglect it, for nothing less than your
whole heart is the devotion due. To give it less than
your whole heart is truly to insult God, and to insult
the subject of salvation.

What shall we think of those who seem never to
make any progress at all? Is it not very plain that
they give much less than their whole hearts to this

matter? It is most certain that if they gave their whole hearts intelligently to it, they would make progress— would speedily find their way to Christ. To make no progress is therefore a decisive indication of having no real heart in this pursuit. How can such escape, seeing they neglect so great salvation?

5

BELIEVING WITH THE HEART

"For with the heart man believeth unto righteousness."—*Romans* x. 10

THE subject brought to view in this passage requires of us, that we should,

I. Distinguish carefully between intellectual and heart-faith.

There are several different states of mind which are currently called *faith*, this term being obviously used in various senses. So, also, is the term *heart* used in various senses, and, indeed, there are but few terms which are not used with some variety of signification. Hence it becomes very important to discriminate.

Thus, in regard to faith, the Scriptures affirm that the "devils also believe and tremble," but it surely cannot be meant that they have heart-faith. They do not "believe unto righteousness".

Faith in the intellect is a judgment—an opinion. The mind so judges, and is convinced that the facts are so. Whatever the nature of the things believed, this is an involuntary state of mind. Those things believed may be truth; they may relate to God and may embrace the great fundamental facts and doctrines of religion; yet this faith may not result in righteousness. It is often true that persons have their judgments convinced, yet this conviction reaches not beyond their intelligence. Or perhaps it may go so much further as to move their feelings and play on their sensibility, and yet may do nothing more. It may produce no change in the *will*. It may result in no new moral purpose; may utterly fail to reach the voluntary attitude of the mind, and, hence, will make no change in the life.

But heart-faith, on the other hand, is true confidence, and involves an earnest committal of one's self and interests to the demands of the truth believed. It is precisely such a trust as we have in those to whom we cling in confidence—such as children feel in their real friends and true fathers and mothers. We know they are naturally ready to believe what is said to them, and to commit themselves to the care of those they love.

The heart is in this. It is a voluntary state of mind —always substantially and essentially an act of the will. This kind of faith will, of course, always affect the feelings, and will influence the *life*. Naturally, it tends towards righteousness, and may truly be said to be "unto righteousness". It implies love, and seems in its very nature to unify itself with the affections. The inspired writers plainly did not hold faith to be so purely an act of will as to exclude the affections. Obviously, they made it *include* the affections.

II. I must now proceed to notice some of the *conditions of intellectual faith*.

1.   Sometimes, but not always, faith of the heart is essential to faith of the intellect. Thus, it may be necessary that we have heart-faith in a man before we are duly prepared to investigate the facts that relate to his character. So, in relation to God, if we lack heart-faith in him, we are in no state to deal fairly with the evidence of his works and ways. Here it is well to notice the vast difference between the irresistible assumptions of the mind respecting God, and those things which we arrive at by study and reasoning. Heart-faith seems essential to any candid investigation.

2.   It is also essential to our *conviction* as to the truth. I am not prepared to judge candidly concerning a friend, unless I have some of this heart-faith in him. Suppose I hear a rumour about my best friend, affirming something which is deeply scandalous. My regard for him forbids my believing this scandalous report, unless it comes most fully sustained by testimony. On the other hand, if I had no heart-confidence in him, my intelligence might be thrown entirely off and I might do both him and myself the greatest injustice.

Many of you have had this experience in regard to faith. Often, in the common walks of life, you have found that, if it had not been for your heart-confidence, you would have been greatly deceived. Your heart held on ; at length, the evidence shone out ; you were in a condition to judge charitably, and thus you arrived at the truth.

3.   Heart-faith is specially essential where there is mystery. Of course there are points in religious doc-

trine which are profoundly mysterious. This fact is not peculiar to religious truth, but is common to every part of God's works—which is equivalent to saying, It is common to all real science. Any child can ask me questions which I cannot answer. Without heart-confidence, it would be impossible for society to exist. Happily for us, we can often wisely confide when we cannot, by any means, understand.

In the nature of the case, there must be mysteries about God, for the simple reason that he is infinite and we are finite. Yet he reveals enough of himself to authorise us to cherish the most unbounded confidence in him. Therefore, let no one stumble at this, as though it were some strange thing; for, in fact, the same thing obtains to some extent in all our social relations. In these, we are often compelled to confide in our friends where the case seems altogether suspicious. Yet we confide, and, by-and-by, the truth comes to light, and we are thankful that our heart-faith held us from doing them injustice.

4. Again, heart-faith is specially in place where there is contradictory evidence.

Often it may seem to you that God must be partial. Then the mind needs the support of confidence in God. You go on safely if there is, underlying all, the deep conviction that God is and must be right. See that woman, stripped of everything—husband, children, all; —how can she give any account of this? You may remember the case of a woman who travelled West with her husband and family ; there buried her husband and all but two little ones, and then made her weary way back with these on foot. Pinching want and weariness drove her into a stranger's dwelling at night-fall; there a churlish man would have turned her into the street, but his wife had a human heart, and insisted on letting them stay, even if she herself sat up all night. Think on the trying case of that lone widow. She does not sleep; her mingled grief and faith find utterance in the words, "*My heart is breaking, but God is good!*"

How could she make it out that God is good? Just as you would in the case of your husband, if one should tell you he had gone for ever, and proved faithless to his vows. You can set this insinuation aside, and let your heart rise above it. You do this on the strength of your heart-faith.

So the Christian does in regard to many mysterious points in God's character and ways. You cannot see how God can exist without even beginning to exist; or how he can exist in three persons, since no other beings known to you exist in more than one. You cannot see how he can be eternally good, and yet suffer sin and misery to befall his creatures. But, with heart-faith, we do not need to have everything explained. The heart says to its Heavenly Father, I do not need to catechise thee, nor ask impertinent questions, for I know it is all right. I know God can never do anything wrong. And so the soul finds a precious joy in trusting, without knowing how the mystery is solved. Just as a wife, long parted from her husband, and, under circumstances that need explanation, yet when he returns, she rushes to meet him with her loving

welcome, without waiting for one word of explanation.
Suppose she had waited for the explanation before she
could speak a kind word. This might savour of the
intellect, but certainly it would not do honour to her
heart. For her heart-confidence, her husband loves
her better than ever, and well he may!

You can understand this; and can you not also apply
it to your relations to God? God may appear to your
view to be capricious, but you know he is not; may
appear unjust, but you know he cannot be. Ah,
Christian, when you comprehend the fact of God's
wider reach of vision, and of his greater love, then
you will cry out, with Job, "Though he slay me,
yet will I trust in him". When you have trusted so,
think you not that your heart will be as dear to Christ
as ever?

III. Let us next consider *what are not, and what
are, conditions of heart-faith.*

1. It is *not* conditioned upon comprehending the
facts to be believed. We may know a thing to be a
fact, while yet we are entirely unable to explain it. The
reasons and the explanations are quite a different thing
from the evidence which sustains the fact, and commends it to our belief.

2. Let it also be borne in mind that it is not half
as necessary to know all the reasons in the case of
God's ways as in man's. The ground of the difference is, that we know, in general, that God is always
right—a knowledge which we cannot have in regard to
man. Of God, our deepest and most resistless convictions assure us that all is right. Our corresponding

convictions in the case of man are far from being irresistible. Yet, even in regard to men, we often find
that a conviction of their rectitude, which is far less
than irresistible, leads us to trust. How much more
should our stronger convictions as to God lead us
evermore to trust in him !

3. Again this heart-faith in God does not rest on
our ability to prove even that God exists. Many an
earnest Christian has never thought of this, any more
than of proving his own existence. An irresistible conviction gives him both, without other proof.

But, positively, God must be revealed to your inner
being so that you are conscious of his existence and
presence. There is not, perhaps, in the universe, a
thing of which we can be more certain than of God's
existence. The mind may be more deeply acquainted
with God than with any other being or thing. Hence
this heart-confidence may be based on God's revelations to the inner soul of man. Such revelations may
reach the very highest measure of certainty. I do not
mean to imply here that we are not certain of the facts
of observation. But this is a stronger assurance and
certainty. The mind becomes personally acquainted
with God, and is conscious of this direct and positive
knowledge.

4. A further condition is, that the soul be inwardly
drawn to God. In our relations to each other, we are
sometimes conscious of a peculiar sympathy which
draws us towards a friend. This fact is a thing of consciousness, of which we may be quite unable to give
any explanation. A similar attraction draws us to

God, and seems to be a natural condition of the strongest forms of heart-faith.

5. It is quite essential to heart-faith that we have genuine love to God. In the absence of good-will towards God, there never can be this faith of the heart. The wife has no heart-faith in her husband, save as she loves him. Her heart must be drawn to him in real love— else his heart-faith will draw back and demand more evidence.

In view of this principle, God takes measures to win our love and draw our hearts to himself. As human beings do towards each other, so *he* manifests his deep interest in us—pours out his blessings on us in lavish profusion, and, in every way, strives to assure us that he is truly our friend. These are his methods to win the confidence of our hearts. When it becomes real to us that we owe everything to God,—our health, gifts, all our comforts,—then we can bear many dark and trying things. Then we know that God loves us, even though he scourge us ; just as children know that parents love them, and mean their good, even though they chastise them. Under these broad and general manifestations of love, they confide, even though there be no present manifestations of love. You may remember how Cecil taught his little daughter the meaning of gospel faith. She came to him, one day, with her hands full of little beads, greatly delighted, to show them. He said to her calmly, " You had better throw them all into the fire ". She was almost confounded ; but, when she saw he was in earnest, she trustfully obeyed, and cast them in. After a few days, he brought home for her a casket of jewels. "There," said he, "my daughter, you had faith in me the other day, and threw your beads into the fire ; that was *faith ;* now I can give you things much more precious. Are not these far better?" So you should always believe in God. He has jewels for those who will believe, and cast away their sins.

IV. Again, I observe, *heart-faith is unto righteousness*—real obedience. This trustful and affectionate state of heart naturally leads us to obey God. I have often admired the faith manifested by the old theologian philosophers who held fast to their confidence in God, despite of the greatest of absurdities. Their faith could laugh at the most absurd principles involved in their philosophy of religious truth. It is a remarkable fact that the greater part of the church have been in their philosophy *necessitarians*, holding not the freedom, but the bondage, of the will ;—their doctrine being that the will is determined *necessarily* by the strongest motive. President Edwards held these philosophical views, but despite of them, he believed that God is supremely good ; the absurdities of this philosophy did not shake his faith in God. So all the really Old School theologians hold the absurdities of hyper-Calvinism ; as, for example, that God absolutely and supremely controls all the moral actions of all his creatures.

Dr Beecher, in controversy with Dr. Wilson, some years since, held that obligation implied ability to obey. This Dr. Wilson flatly denied. Whereupon Dr. B. remarked that few men could march up and face such a proposition without winking. It is often the case that men have such heart-confidence in God that they will trust him despite of the most flagrant absurdities. There is less superstition in this than I used to suppose, and more faith. Men forget their dogmas and philosophy, and, despite of both, love and confide.

Some men have held monstrous doctrines—even that God is the author of sin, and puts forth his divine efficiency to make men sin, as truly as, by his Spirit, to make them holy. This view was held by Dr. Emmons; yet he was eminently a pious man, of childlike, trustful spirit. It is indeed strange how such men could hold these absurdities at all, and, scarcely less so, how they could hold them and yet confide sweetly in God. Their hearts must have been fixed in this faith by some other influence than that of these monstrous notions in philosophy and theology. For these views of God, we absolutely know, were contrary to their *reason*, though not to their *reasonings*—a very wide and essential distinction, which is sometimes overlooked. The intuitive affirmations of their reason were one thing; the points which they reached by their philosophical reasonings were quite another thing. The former could not lie about God, the latter could. The former laid that sure foundation for heart-faith; the latter went to make up their intellectual notions, the absurdities of which (we notice with admiration), never seemed to shake their Christian faith. While these reasonings pushed them on into the greatest absurdities, their reason held their faith and piety straight.

The faith of the heart is proof against all forms of infidelity. Without this, nothing is proof. For if men without piety drop the affirmations of their intuitive reason, and then attempt, philosophically, to reason out all the difficulties they meet with, they almost inevitably stumble.

Heart-faith carries one over the manifold mysteries and difficulties of God's providence. In this field there must be difficulties, for no human vision can penetrate to the bottom of God's providential plans and purposes.

So, also, does this faith of the heart carry one over the mysteries of the atonement. It is indeed curious to notice how the heart gets over all these. It is generally the case that the atonement is accepted by the heart unto salvation, before its philosophy is understood. It was manifestly so with the apostles; so with their hearers; and so, even with those who heard the Lord Jesus Christ himself. The Bible says but very little indeed on the point of the *philosophy* of the atonement.

So, also, of the doctrine of the Trinity; and so of other doctrines generally. They were known and taught as practical truths, and were accepted as such, long before their philosophy was specially investigated. If any difficulties arose in minds specially inquisitive, it was overcome by heart-faith, or settled by the intuitive affirmations of the reason, and not by speculative reasoning.

It is in no sense unreasonable that God should require us to have such faith in him. Properly consid-

ered, he does not require us to believe what we do
not know to be true. He does not ask us to renounce
our common sense, and exercise a groundless credulity.
When we trust his general character, and accept certain dark dispensations of providence as doubtless
right, what is it that we believe? Not the special
reason for this mysterious dispensation, but we believe
that, despite of its dark aspect to us, God's hand in it
is both wise and good, and we believe this because
we have abundant ground to confide in his general
character. It is as if you were to tell me that a known
and tried friend of mine had told a lie. I should say,
" I cannot believe it. I know him too well." But you
say, " Here is the evidence. It looks very dark against
him." "Very likely," I reply, "but yet I cannot believe it. There will be some explanation of this. I
cannot believe it."

Now I consider myself fully authorised to reject at
once all surmises and rumours against my known friend.
I am bound to do so, until the evidence against him
becomes absolutely conclusive. This is altogether rea-
sonable. How much more so in the case of dark
things in God's doings !

For it should be considered that man may deceive
us ; God never can. We do not know man's heart always, to the very core ; and if we did, it may change ;
what once was true, becomes false. But not so with
God : our intuitive convictions affirm that God is always
good, and always wise ; and, moreover, that there can
never be any declension in his love, or any revolution
in his character.

Consequently Christians are often called on to believe God, not only without, but against, present evidence.

Abraham, called out of his home and country to go into a strange land, obeyed, not knowing whither he went. He might have asked many questions about the reasons; he does not appear to have asked any.

Commanded to offer up Isaac, he might, with apparent propriety, have expostulated earnestly. He might have said, "Lord, that would be murder! It would outrage the natural affection which thou hast planted in my bosom. It would encourage the heathen around us in their horrid abominations of making their children pass through the fire to Moloch." All this, and more, he might have said; but, so far as appears, he said nothing—save this: " The Lord commands, and I obey. If he pleases he can raise up my Isaac from the dead." So he went on and virtually offered up his son Isaac, and, "in a figure, received him again from the dead". And God fixed the seal of his approbation on this act of faith, and held it out before all ages as a model of faith and obedience, despite of darkness and objections.

So Christians are often called to believe without present evidence, other than what comes from their knowledge of God's general character. For a season, God lets everything go against them, yet they believe. Said a woman, passing through great trials, with great confidence in God: "O Lord, I know thou art good, for thou hast shown me this; but, Lord, others do not understand this; they are stumbled at it. Canst thou not show them so that they shall understand this?"

CONCLUSION

1. The demand for reasons often embarrasses our faith. This is one of the tricks of the devil. He would embarrass our faith by telling us we must understand all God's ways before we believe. Yet we ought to see that this is impossible and unreasonable. Abraham could not see the reasons for God's command to offer Isaac a bloody sacrifice; he might have expostulated; but he did not. The simplicity and beauty of his faith appears all along in this very thing—that *he raised no questions.* He had a deeper insight into God's character. He knew too much of God to question his wisdom or his love. For, a man might understand all the reasons of God's ways, yet this knowledge might do him no good; his heart might rebel even then.

In this light you may see why so much is said about Abraham's faith. It was gloriously trustful and unquestioning! What a model! No wonder God commends it to the admiring imitation of the world!

2. It is indeed true that faith must often go forward in the midst of darkness. Who can read the histories of believing saints, as recorded in Scripture, without seeing that faith often leads the way through trials? It would be but a sorry development of faith, if, at every step, God's people must know everything before they could trust him, and must understand all his reasons. Most ample grounds for faith lie in his general character, so that we do not need to understand the special reasons for his particular acts.

3. We are mere infants—miserably poor students of God's ways. His dealings on every side of us appear to us mysterious. Hence it should be expected that we shall fail to comprehend his reasons, and consequently we must confide in him without this knowledge. Indeed, just here lies the virtue of faith, that it trusts God on the ground of his general character, while the mind can by no means comprehend his reasons for particular acts. Knowing enough of God to assure us that he must be good, our faith trusts him, although the special evidence of goodness in particular cases may be wanting.

This is a kind of faith which many do not seem to possess or to understand. Plainly they do not confide in God's dealings.

4. It is manifestly needful that God should train Christians to exercise faith here and now; since in heaven we shall be equally unable to comprehend all his dealings. The holy in heaven will no doubt believe in God; but they must do it by simple faith—not on the ground of a perfect knowledge of God's plans. What a trial of faith it must have been to the holy in heaven to see sin enter our world! They could see few, perhaps none, of the reasons, before the final judgment, and must have fallen back upon the intuitive affirmations of their own minds. The utmost they could say was, We know God must be good and wise; therefore we must wait to see the results, and humbly *trust.*

5. It is not best for parents to explain everything to their children, and, especially, they should not take

the ground of requiring nothing of which they cannot explain all the reasons. Some profess to take this ground. It is, for many reasons, unwise. God does not train his children so.

Faith is really natural to children. Yet some will not believe their children converted until they can be real theologians. This assumes that they must have all the great facts of the gospel system explained so that they can comprehend their philosophy before they believe them. Nothing can be further from the truth.

6. It sometimes happens that those who are converted in childhood become students of theology in more advanced years, and then, getting proud of their philosophy and wisdom, lose their simple faith and relapse into infidelity. Now I do not object to their studying the philosophy of every doctrine up to the limits of human knowledge; but I do object to their casting away their faith in God. For there is no lack of substantial testimony to the great doctrines of the gospel. Their philosophy may stagger the wisest man; but the evidence of their truth ought to satisfy all, and alike the child and the philosopher. Last winter I was struck with this fact—which I mention because it seems to present one department of the evidences of Christianity in a clear light. One judge of the court said to another, I come to you with my assertion that I inwardly know Jesus Christ, and as truly and as well as I know you. Can you reject such testimony? What would the people of this State say to you if you rejected such testimony on any other subject? Do you not every day let men testify to their

own experience? The judge replied, "I cannot answer you".

"Why, then," replied the other, "do you not believe this testimony? I can bring before you thousands who will testify to the same thing."

7. Again I remark, it is of great use to study the truths of the gospel system theologically and philosophically, for thus you may reach a satisfactory explanation of many things which your heart knew, and clave to, and would have held fast till the hour of your death. It is a satisfaction to you, however, to see the beautiful harmony of these truths with each other, and with the known laws of mind and of all just government.

Yet theological students sometimes decline in their piety, and for a reason which it were well for them to understand. One enters upon this study simple-hearted and confiding; but, by-and-by, study expands his views; he begins to be charmed with the explanations he is able to give of many things not understood before; becomes opinionated and proud; becomes ashamed of his former simple heart-faith, and thus stumbles fearfully, if not fatally. If you will hold on with all your simple heart-confidence to the immutable love and wisdom of God, all will be well. But it never can be well to put your intellectual philosophy in the place of the simplicity of gospel faith.

8. Herein is seen one reason why some students do not become pious. They determine that they will understand everything before they become Christians. Of course they are never converted. Quite in point,

here, is a case I saw a few years since. Dr. B., an intelligent but not pious man, had a pious wife, who was leading her little daughter to Christ. The Doctor, seeing this, said to her, Why do you try to lead that child to Christ? I cannot understand these things myself, although I have been trying to understand them these many years; how, then, can she? But some days after as he was riding out alone, he began to reflect on the matter; the truth flashed upon his mind, and he saw that neither of them could understand God unto perfection—not he any more than his child; while yet either of them could know enough to believe unto salvation.

9. Again, gospel faith is voluntary—a will-trust. I recollect a case in my own circle of friends. I could not satisfy my mind about one of them. At length, after long struggling, I said, I will repel these things from my mind, and rule out these difficulties. My friend is honest and right; I will believe it, and will trust him none the less for these slanders. In this I was right.

Towards God this course is always right. It is always right to cast away from your mind all those dark suspicious about him who can never make mistakes, and who is too good to purpose wrong. I once said to a sister in affliction, Can you not believe all this is for your good, though you cannot see *how* it is? She brightened up, saying: " I must believe in God, and I will ".

Who of you have this heart-faith? Which of you will now commit yourself to Christ? If the thing required were intellectual faith, I could explain to you how it is reached. It must be through searching the evidence in the case. But heart-faith must be reached by simple effort—by a voluntary purpose to *trust*. Ye who say, I cannot do this, bow your knees before God and commit yourself to his will; say, "O my Saviour! I take thee at thy word". This is a simple act of will.

6

THE RICH MAN AND LAZARUS

" There was a certain rich man, which was clothed in purple and fine linen, and fared sumptuously every day: and there was a certain beggar named Lazarus, which was laid at his gate, full of sores, and desiring to be fed with the crumbs which fell from the rich man's table: moreover, the dogs came and licked his sores.

" And it came to pass, that the beggar died, and was carried by the angels into Abraham's bosom. The rich man also died, and was buried: and in hell he lifted up his eyes, being in torments, and seeth Abraham afar off, and Lazarus in his bosom. And he cried, and said, Father Abraham, have mercy on me, and send Lazarus, that he may dip the tip of his finger in water, and cool my tongue; for I am tormented in this flame. But Abraham said, Son, remember that thou in thy lifetime receivedst thy good things, and likewise Lazarus evil things: but now he is comforted, and thou art tormented. And besides all this, beween us and you there is a great gulf fixed; so that they which would pass from hence to you, cannot; neither can they pass to us, that would come from thence.

" Then he said, I pray thee therefore, father, that thou wouldest send him to my father's house: for I have five brethren; that he may testify unto them, lest they also come into this place of torment. Abraham saith unto him, They have Moses and the prophets; let them hear them. And he said, Nay, father Abraham; but if one went unto them from the dead, they will repent. And he said unto him, If they hear not Moses and the prophets, neither will they be persuaded, though one rose from the dead."—*Luke* xvi. 19-31

A PARABLE is a little anecdote or a case of supposed history, designed to illustrate some truth. A simple and striking mode of illustration—it makes no attempt at reasoning; indeed, it takes the place of all reasoning by at once revealing truth to the mind. In general, parables *assume* certain truths—a thing which they have an ample right to do, for some truths need no proof,* and in other cases a teacher may speak from his perfect knowledge, and in such a case, there can be no reason for demanding that he stop to prove all he asserts.

In the case of parables it is often interesting to notice what truths they do assume. This is especially true of the parables of Christ; for none were ever more rich by virtue both of the truths directly taught and also by virtue of the truths they assume. I may also remark here that truths are taught in Christ's parables both directly and incidentally. Some one great truth is the leading object of the illustration, yet other truths of the highest importance may be taught incidentally, not being embraced in his direct design.

The passage which I have read to you this morning, is probably a parable, though not distinctly affirmed to be so. The nature of the case seems to show this; although these very circumstances might have all actually occurred in fact and in the same order as here related.

In discussing the passage, I propose,

I. To notice some truths that are assumed in it;

II. To present some that are intentionally taught.

I. 1. Christ assumes in this passage the direct *opposite* of *annihilation*. He assumes that men are *not* annihilated at death, nor indeed ever. For he speaks of things that take place immediately after death. The men who lived on earth live beyond death, and receive according to the things they have done here in the body. It was no part of his direct object to *affirm* this doctrine ; yet his statements imply it. Being himself *the Great Teacher*, it is not without reason that he should assume the fundamental truths that pertain to man's future existence under God's moral government.

2. He assumes that the state into which both good and bad men pass at death is one of real and intense *consciousness*. This of course denies the assumption that this state is an unconscious one. You are aware that some who do not hold to annihilation, yet hold to unconsciousness in the intermediate state between death and the resurrection. This doctrine, whether applied to saints or sinners, is entirely set aside by our Saviour's teachings in this narrative.

3. He assumes that the righteous and the wicked recognise each other after death. The rich man knew both Abraham and Lazarus. Abraham knew him. They all respectively knew each other. The statements represent the colloquy to have been held between the rich man and Abraham. Abraham, though long since in heaven, knew both this rich man and Lazarus. It was not our Lord's design directly to affirm this, yet he obviously implies it.

4. It is also assumed that they are acquainted with each other's state and history. All these matters were entirely familiar to their minds.

5. It is fully assumed that at death the righteous go immediately to a state of bliss and the wicked to a place of torment. This lies out undeniably on the face of the passage.

II. I am next to notice some of the truths distinctly and directly *taught* in this passage.

1. That at death angels conduct the righteous to their place of blessedness. It is expressly said of Lazarus that he was carried by angels into Abraham's bosom. Dogs were his companions here up to his death : angels immediately thereafter. When the dogs could minister to his wants no longer, angels stepped in and took his case in charge. They bore him away to the home of the blessed.

We may infer that this is the common employment of angels. Paul in Hebrews i. 12 strengthens this position, in his question, "Are they not all ministering spirits, sent forth to minister for them who shall be heirs of salvation ? "

2. Saints after death are sensible of no want. They have nothing left to desire. They are sensible of wanting nothing that can be needful to their highest happiness. In this life they may have had their cup filled with bitterest grief; but at death, this cup is removed for ever away, and quite another cup is placed to their lips—for ever. Lazarus had his evil things in this world : poverty, pain, sores, and want were his portion here ; but, after death, he knew these things no more at all. They passed away for ever.

3. On the other hand, sinners after death are full of want, and have no good at all. The rich man asked

for only the very smallest favour. He *had* fared sumptuously every day ; but now he is reduced *so low* he can only beg for one drop of water to cool his tongue. He asks for only so much as might adhere to the tip of one's finger when taken from the water. You have seen persons lie under a burning fever—prostrate, parched, can't say a word, can only beckon for water —water—one drop to cool their burning tongue. See the man dying ;—he tries to move a little, towards the water ; ah, he fails ; he sinks back in his bed for the last time, and the burning fever has used up all his strength. You who have suffered from fever know what this means—to have a consuming fire shut up within you. Here mark. The Great Teacher makes the rich man cry out, " Send Lazarus, that he may dip the tip of his finger in water, and cool my tongue ; for I am tormented in this flame ". Why did he not ask for an ocean of water, or a pail-full at least, or a pitcher-full ? why restrict himself to the least drop ? Plainly he knew himself to be placed *beyond all good.* He knew this was the utmost he could ask, and even this is denied him ! What could our Lord have designed but to teach this ? How irresistibly is this taught and with what overpowering force ! What remarkable facts are these ! How obviously and how forcibly is the truth taught here that saints at death pass into a state all joyful, but the wicked into one of unutterable torment !

4. We learn the state of mind in which the wicked are. This man asks for only the very slightest mitigation. He says not one word about *pardon ;* this he knows to be impossible. How small the boon he

dares to ask! How very small, if he could have had
it, would have been the boon of one small drop of
water on a tongue tormented in flame. Yet he does
not dare to ask for anything beyond this;—nor even
this of God! He knew and he most deeply felt that
he had cast off God, and God in turn had cast off him.
He could not think of speaking to God. He could
venture to speak only to Abraham; and this solitary
Bible case of prayer to saints in heaven surely affords
no very plausible foundation for the Romish practice.
This rich man had not the least hope of release from
his woe. He did not ask so great a boon as this.
Deep in his soul he felt that such a request was for
ever precluded.

It is remarkable, too, that, though the boon he did
ask was so trifling and his need so great, yet even this
pittance was denied him. Abraham gave him plainly
to understand that this was impossible. Son, said he,
remember that thou in thy lifetime hast received thy
good things; thou hast had thine *all;* there are no
more for thee to enjoy!

5. Besides this, there is a great gulf fixed—parting
for ever the saved from the damned: we cannot go to
you if we would; you cannot come to us, however
much you may desire it. Most plainly does Christ
teach in this representation that the state of both the
righteous and the wicked is fixed, fixed for ever, and
for ever changeless. There can be no passage open,
therefore, as some would fain have it, from one world
to the other. They who are in heaven can never get
to hell to help the suffering ones there if they would;

and, on the other hand, the miserable in hell can never get to heaven. What less than this could the Saviour have intended to teach—that each class enter at death upon another state which is to each alike unchangeable? The righteous cannot pass the great gulf to hell ; the wicked, cannot pass it to heaven. Once heaven's gate was open to even the sinner on his repentance. Now it is open to him no more. He has passed away from the world where his moral state can be changed. He has entered on one where no change can reach him any more at all for ever.

6. The wicked dread to have their friends come to them in this place of torment. You see this feeling most distinctly manifested in this parable. The reason of the feeling is obvious. They are still human beings, and therefore it can be no joy to them to have their earthly friends come into their place of woe. They have human feelings. They know they can look for no alleviation of their own woe from the presence of their friends. They know that if those friends come there as they did they can never escape ; therefore they beg that those friends may never come. Therefore this rich man prays that Abraham would send Lazarus to his five brethren, to testify to them, lest they also come into that place of torment.

7. The state of mind that rejects the Bible would reject any testimony that could be given. This is plainly taught here, and can be proved. It can be proved that the testimony of one who should rise from the dead is no better or stronger than that of the Bible. Paul said he had been caught up to the third heaven,

but men would not believe him. Or take the case of
Lazarus, raised beyond all question from the dead. We
are not told what he taught, nor is it said that his instructions made any special impressions on the living
unbelievers of that generation. Those of you who have
read the history of William Tennant—a co-labourer
with Whitfield and Edwards, know how he apparently
died ; how after death he went to heaven ; how he, too,
like Paul, saw there unspeakable things which no man
could utter ; how he returned again, and lived several
years as one who had seen the glories of heaven ;
but was this stronger evidence than the Bible itself?
Did it surpass in strength of demonstration the teachings of Moses and of the prophets? Yet more, did it
surpass the force and evidence with which Jesus spake,
and also his apostles ? No, verily. When unbelief has
taken possession of the mind, you may pile miracle on
miracle ; men will not believe it. Suppose ever so
many should rise from the dead. Men who reject the
Bible would not believe their testimony. They would
insist either that they had not been really dead, or that,
if they had been, they did not bring back a reliable report from that other country. They would make a
thousand objections, as they do now against the
Bible, and with much more plausibility then than now.
Now, they only know their objections are really un-
founded ; then they would have more plausible objections to make, and would be sure to give them credit
enough to refuse to repent under their teachings. They
would not be persuaded even then.

8. The estimation in which God holds men may

not be learned from their outward circumstances. His favour cannot be inferred from the trappings of wealth ; nor is it precluded by any amount of poverty. These external things neither prove nor disprove God's approbation of the hearts and the life of men.

9. The righteous need not envy rich sinners. Lazarus did not envy the rich man. He saw that he was petted for his great wealth, but pitied rather than envied him. He doubtless understood that this man was having his good things in this world. So good men, if they have faith, understand that those rich and wicked men are receiving all their good things in this world ; therefore are far from being objects of envy.

10. The former poverty of the righteous poor will give a keener relish to the joys of heaven. Think of the abject poverty of this man—wandering about with no home, no place even to lay his head. So multitudes in Eastern countries may be seen lying around the city walls like the swine of the streets. I saw them in Malta when I was there, and in Sicily also. They had no home to go to, no resources against a sick or stormy day. So Lazarus lived ; and it was from such a life and such scenes that he was transferred to the royal palace of Jehovah. Take the case of some poor beggar lying helpless outside the palace-walls of Queen Victoria. Suppose him suddenly taken up and exalted to the highest honours of the palace itself. How would his joy intoxicate his brain—too much for flesh and blood to bear ! So poor saints passing from the dunghill on earth to the golden palaces of heaven. It is well they lose their nerves in the change, for surely nerves of

flesh could not bear so great a change. See Lazarus, sick and sore, perhaps putrid—licked by dogs ; but he reached at length the crisis of his sorrows, and all suddenly the mortal coil drops, and his spirit takes wings —angels receive him ; he soars away, and heaven opens wide its gates of pearl to make him welcome ! Sometimes when I have stood and seen the Christian die— have seen him struggle and pant and gasp and pass away, I have said, What a wonderful change is this ! See how that eye grows glassy and dark ; then it closes ; it sees no more of earth, but all suddenly it opens on the glories of the upper world, to be closed no more for ever !

11.   But to have the luxuries of this life superseded by the poverty and woe of hell—how awful ! This rich man had royal wealth. We are told that he fared sumptuously every day—not only on special occasions, but every day ! Every day, too, he was clad in purple and fine linen ; but now how wonderful the contrast ! Nothing is said of the burial of Lazarus ; perhaps he had none worth noticing ; but this man had a funeral. It was a noticeable fact. Perhaps thousands gathered round his remains to do him honour—but where is he ? Lifting up his eyes in hell, being in torments ! What a change ! From his table and his palace, to hell ! Lazarus passed from his sores and beggary to heaven ; the rich man, from his pomp and pride and feasting, to hell. As the great poverty of Lazarus, so set off in contrast with heaven, must have given great edge and keenness to the joys of that world, so, on the reverse scale, how dreadful the contrast which this rich man experienced !

If we always get clearer and stronger views by contrast, surely we have a picture drawn here that is adapted to teach us awful truth and force it home on the soul with telling power.

12. If it be true that angels convey saints to heaven, as we are taught both here and elsewhere in God's word, then it is not irrational to suppose that what many saints say in their dying hours of the things they see, is strictly true. Gathering darkness clouds the senses, and the mind becomes greatly spiritual, as their looks plainly show. Those looks—the eye, the countenance, the melting whisper, these tell the story better than any words can do it; indeed, no words can describe those *looks*—no language can paint what you can stand by and see and hear—a peace so deep and so divine; this shows that the soul is *almost* in heaven. In all ages it has been common for some dying saints to hear music which they supposed to be of heaven, and to see angels near and around them. With eyes that see what others cannot see, they recognise their attending angels as already come. "Don't *you* hear that music?" say they. "Don't you see those shinning ones? they come, they come!" But attending friends are yet too carnal to see such objects and to hear such sounds; for it is the mind, and not the body, that has eyes. It is the mind that sees, and not the body. No doubt, in such cases, they do really see angelic forms and hear angelic voices. The Bible says, "Precious in the sight of the Lord is the death of his saints." How gloriously do these closing scenes illustrate this truth!

13. If this be true of saints, then doubtless wicked

spirits are allowed to drag the wicked down from their dying beds to hell. Nor is it unreasonable to suppose that they, too, really see awful shapes and hear dreadful sounds. "Who is that weeping and wailing? Did I not hear a groan? Is there not some one weeping as if in awful agony? Oh, that awful thing! take him away, *take him away!* He will seize me and drag me down; take him away, *away!*"

So the wicked are sometimes affected in their dying moments. There is no good reason to doubt that these objects seen and sounds heard, by saints and sinners in their last earthly moments, are realities. You who have read Dr. Nelson's book on infidelity, cannot but have noticed especially what he says of the experience of persons near death. These things passed under his observation chiefly while he was a physician, and while yet an infidel himself. Dying sinners would cry out, "Oh, that awful creature! take him away, away! why don't you take him away?" Ye who know Dr. Nelson, must have known that he did not say these things at random. He did not admit them without evidence, or state them without due consideration.

14. We are left to infer the character of this rich man from his worldly-mindedness. Christ did not seem to deem it necessary to state that he was a wicked man, but left this to be inferred from his self-indulgent life. He needed only to say of him that he lived for *self-gratification;* that he used his wealth for himself only, and not for the good of man, or for the glory of God. This explained his character sufficiently.

People act very much in this world as if they supposed poverty would disqualify them for heaven. They would seem to hold the exact opposite of the truth. Christ said, " How hardly shall a rich man enter into the kingdom of heaven " ; and yet, who seems to have the least fear of losing heaven by means of the snare of wealth ? How wonderful is the course that men pursue, and indeed a great many Christian men are pursuing ! A Christian mother, writing to me from New York, said, " All, even Christians, are giving themselves up to making *money*, MONEY, MONEY ! They are wholly given up to stocks, and banks, and getting rich." There is a great deal of this spirit all over the country, and even here. · But look at it in the light of this parable and of our Saviour's assumption in regard to the character of this rich man, and what a fearful state is this to live and to die in !

15. What can Universalists say or believe when they read such passages as this ? What miserable shifts they must make to interpret these words ! I recollect when I tried and wanted to be Universalist, and for this purpose went to their meetings and heard their arguments, I said to myself, " For very shame, I could never use such arguments ; no, not for the shame of admitting and avowing such absurdities ! " What can be more absurd than to resort to such sophistry and special pleading to set aside statements so clear and direct to the point as these in this chapter !

God is giving to all sinners—to you sinners in this place—a great many rich gifts. What use are you making of them ? What are you doing with these gifts ? What are you doing with these things which

God comes down each day to bring to you? Are you cavilling, to prevent Christ from saving you if you can? Many act as if they meant to avoid being saved if by any means they can. You act just like reprobates.— But I must explain myself. I often meet with persons whose spirit makes me believe they are reprobates. You know that all things are eternally present to the mind of God. He saw how these sinners would treat the gospel. He saw they would repel and hate Christ— would not love his service nor accept the offers of his great salvation. He saw all this in his past eternity: therefore He reprobated them; therefore He gave them over to their own hearts' lusts. Those things which God saw in the depths of his eternity, we only see as they boil up upon the surface of actual present life. You see them resist the Spirit; you see them cavil and fight against God's truth; you know they are fighting against God. So strongly does the conviction fasten on the minds of Christians in some cases, that they cannot pray for those who they are assured are reprobates. Said a very pious woman, "For ten years, I have not prayed for that son". Why? She saw that he was set against God, and she could not pray for him. It is indeed an awful thing to find such cases in Christian families. Nobody can tell the agony of a parent's heart to see a son setting at naught all the claims and all the mercies of God, and working his dismal way obstinately down to the depths of an eternal hell. Some of you before me to-day, know that you have children who give awful evidence of being reprobate!

Hear that man across the street sighing as he moves

along. What is the matter? He is in agony for a hardened, reprobate son.

You call at a neighbour's door; you ring the bell; the mother comes. You see the tear in her eye; she can scarcely speak. What is the matter? She has a son, and she fears he is a reprobate. All his conduct heightens the awful fear that he is given over of God.

But let those who have not gone so far, take warning. Some of those whom you have mocked and reviled, you may by-and-by see in glory. They may be in Abraham's bosom, and *you afar off!* You may cry to them for help, but all in vain. Will they rush to your help? No. You see your father, your mother, afar off in that spirit land,—you think they will fly to succour you, and bring you at least one drop of water,— they used to do so many a time when you were in pain. Ah! many a time has that mother watched over your suffering frame, and rushed to your relief; but will she do so now? "My son, hear this: there is no passing from this place to that. You once lived in my house and lay in my bosom, but I cannot bring you one drop of water now!" And has it come to this? Must it come to this? Ah, yes, it *must come to this!*

Christian parents, one word to you. Suppose you conceive of this as your case. You see one of your children crying, "Oh, give me one drop of water to cool my burning tongue!" I know what Universalists would say to this. They say, "Can a parent be happy, and see this? And do you think a parent is more compassionate than God?"

But in that hour of retribution, those Christian

parents will say even of the sons and daughters they have borne, " Let them perish, they are the enemies of God and of his kingdom ! Let them perish, since they *would* not have salvation ! They must perish, for God's throne must stand, and ought to stand, though all the race go down to hell ! "

7

THE WANTS OF MAN

"He began to be in want."—*Luke* xv. 14

"Blessed are they who hunger and thirst after righteousness, for they shall be filled."—*Matthew* v. 6

THE parable of the prodigal son is intended to illustrate the case of the sinner, coming to himself, opening his eyes to his true condition, and feeling himself destitute, empty, and wretched.

Man, as he stands revealed to himself in consciousness, is a wonderful being. By the earliest teachings of consciousness he finds himself to be a duality, consisting of body and soul. Farther revelations made in consciousness show him to be in some respects a tri-unity. For example, he has three classes of mental attributes, sensibility, intellect, and will. Still further, and yet more important in its bearings, he finds himself a tri-unity, inasmuch as he has three sides to his nature,—one related to the material universe around him ; another to all objects of thought and knowledge ; and still another, related to God and to duty.

1. He has first a *body*, and, through this, peculiar relations to the world he lives in. He has appetites for food, and numerous wants that terminate on the physical universe. These wants crave their appropriate

supplies, and cannot be satisfied with anything else. In the order of time, these are earliest developed. They are few in number,—that is, they *may* be,—and those which are real are so. This class alone cease at death. Yet while they exist, they must be supplied.

Another fact deserving notice in reference to this class of wants is that man immediately assumes the existence of the objects to which his physical wants are correlated. The infant assumes this by instinct. There is no need that you should prove to man that these objects exist. He assumes this, and has only to inquire where they may be found. By a necessity of his nature he assumes their existence, and sets himself forthwith to search for them.

2. In the next place, let it be noticed that man has also an intellectual nature. He is made capable of knowledge, and has also an intense desire to know These are real wants of his being. God has provided for their supply in the illimitable ocean of truth which invests him on every side. God has also breathed into his soul a spirit of inquiry, and acting out its deep impulses, he must inquire into the truth and reason of things. It is curious to notice the difference between children and other animals. If you had never seen an infant before, and were to study his developments for the first time, you would be forcibly struck with these remarkable traits. The little one begins to notice, and to look inquiringly, almost as soon as it begins to look at all. See him fix his eyes upon his little hands, as if he would ask, What are these? He looks into his mother's eye as if he would ask a thousand questions, long

before he can utter a word. But you can find no such manifestations of thought and inquiry in the kitten and the lamb. Give them enough to eat and scope for rest and play, and they are satisfied. They will never seem to ask you the reasons of things. Nay more, you cannot awaken within them a spirit of inquiry by any appliances you can employ. It is not in them, and you cannot get it in.

But the infant is a philosopher by birth. He has intellectual wants lying in his very nature, and he cannot be satisfied without their supply. He must know the reasons of things. This is the true idea of philosophy. The lower animals will lie down perfectly satisfied without knowing the reasons of things, or anything more about things than just suffices to meet their animal wants. But man, even from infancy, has wants pressing upon him in this direction, and he rouses himself, like a lion from his lair, to grasp the good his inner being craves in this direction. He cannot be satisfied without. He finds himself related to the whole universe of matter, and oh, what a world is opened to him for inquiry and knowledge! How naturally he looks up and abroad! It is not easy for the horse or the ox to look up. Their eye is prone; but man's is outward and upward. Man is made for inquiry.

It is this spirit of inquiry which leads so many young people to this place. They come here to get knowledge. How they hang on our lips, and press on us for the reasons of things, as if they could not be satisfied till they have penetrated to the bottom of every subject.

Men assume that there is an explanation of everything. They assume that these innate demands for
knowledge were created, not to be denied—not to remain ungratified, but to be gratified. Hence they grasp
after knowledge, searching for it as for silver, and as
if they deemed it more to be desired than gold, yea,
than much fine gold. What young man or young
woman has not felt such curiosity excited, as to extort
the cry, *I must know : I must find out the facts on this
subject, and the reasons of the facts besides !*

3. Thirdly, man has yet another side to his nature—
the moral and spiritual department, correlated to God, to
his attributes and law, and to great questions of duty
and destiny. Man learns from consciousness that he
has such a side to his being—such a department in his
nature. Hence he inquires after God. He raises
questions about right and wrong, and asks to know the
nature of virtue and vice. Often he finds in himself a
great uneasiness of which he cannot well divine the
cause. It puts him upon pressing these inquiries into
his responsibilities and his mission in this state of his
existence.

Let it now be especially observed that man instinc-
tively assumes the existence of those things which stand
related to each of these three sides of his nature. The
infant begins to feel after his food with no thought of
question as to the fact of there being food provided for
his wants. When intelligence opens, the same assumption is made, that there are verities to be known, and
the reasons why these things are so rather than otherwise. In like manner, when the eyes of the moral man

begin to open, he assumes his own immortality, and assumes also the existence of a God. This is, indeed, the true account of his knowledge of this truth. Some have supposed that the idea of God in the human mind is wholly a thing of education. It is so in the same sense in which much of our intellectual knowledge is. There are many things about God which we need to learn from his word and from his works. But no man needs to have it demonstrated to him that there *is* a God, any more than a child needs to have it proved that there is food provided for him in the physical world, or the adult, that there are things to be known. The great cardinal truths pertaining to the existence of God, accountability, and duty, are assumed as readily and surely as men assume that there are truths correlated to their intelligence, or supplies in nature for their animal wants. It is of no use to say that some men are atheists, and therefore this doctrine cannot be true. Some men have, by speculation, befooled themselves into the belief (so they say) that there is no physical universe. But they believe in its existence none the less, and crave the good it proffers, and cannot live without it. Each one of these philosophers, although he may deny the existence of any physical universe, and declare there is no such thing as matter, yet expects his dinner at the appointed hour, and needs it for his comfort full as much as if he had not denied the existence of any such thing. So these atheists only know there is a God, although they say, "*in their heart,*" there is none.

It is vastly difficult for any man to feel at ease while

he is resisting the constitutional demands of any department of his nature. "Alas!" said a young and
ambitious lawyer, who was driving his business and his
books and his briefs,—"alas!" said he, "what is the
matter with me! I try to study, and cannot. I try to
be happy, but I am not. What do I want? Wherein
is the lack that, with all I have, yet leaves me so
wretched?"

It was this strain of inquiry which led him to see
that he needed God for his portion, and could not find
a paradise without him.

Men need not wait for the proof of their immortality, or for proof of the necessity of virtue as a
means for happiness. They know these things by a
spontaneity of their moral nature. They know that
holiness is a great want of their moral nature. How
plainly do they see and know that they need such a
being as God, to love and to obey, to trust and to
adore!

I appeal to these students. If you have cultivated
the habit of self-study, you have learned that you cannot find out yourself without finding God. Tracing
out the problems of your own existence reveals to you
your Maker. An irresistible conviction will force itself
upon you that there is a God, and that you have everything to hope from his favour, and everything to fear
from his frown. A view of yourself and of your own
spiritual wants will show you that nothing else can
supply your need but God. Have you not already
found that the more you study, and the more you cul-
tivate the habit of reflection, the less you can make

yourself happy without God? Most of you find it impossible to enjoy yourselves in sin as you were wont to do before you gave yourselves to thought and reflection. The higher you ascend in the grade of moral and intellectual culture, the more intensely will you feel the want of moral culture and moral enjoyments. It is impossible for you to rise as a man without feeling a growing demand for the presence and influence of God as your Father and Friend.

Commonly, as the human mind opens to surrounding objects, and as its powers successively develop themselves, attention is first turned to physical wants, and next to intellectual. In one or the other of these pursuits, or in both, man is wont to become so engrossed as mainly to overlook the moral side of his nature. Yet the wants of his moral being will develop themselves, often in such a way at first as to make him exceedingly wretched, while yet he does not see what ails him, and quite fails to comprehend the reason of his unhappiness. No amount of knowledge or purely mental culture can make him happy. On the contrary, the more he knows the more he wants, and the more intensely dissatisfied he becomes with himself.

The objects that supply his bodily wants are at hand. He meets them on every side, and in abundance. So, also, pushing his efforts for this end, he finds ample materials for supplying his intellectual wants. He finds enough for mind to feed upon— enough to exercise his faculties, and interest him in studious thought and earnest research.

So, also, with his moral and spiritual wants. These have their correlated objects. God is all around him. In the kingdoms of nature he sees the handiwork of an intelligent, designing Maker; and in the ways of providence, he cannot help seeing the agency of a kind and beneficent Father. As his natural eye gives him the material world, so his spiritual eye would give him God in everything—were it not for the blinding influence of a bad heart. This fearfully darkens his vision to those great spiritual truths he so much needs to know. While he might be advancing hour by hour in the knowledge of God and of spiritual truth, going down into the great depths of sympathy with God, he finds, instead, a fearful conflict between his depraved impulses and his conscience, under the influence of which, truth gains but a slow access to his soul. Moreover, the moral side of his nature being latest developed, he often becomes so engrossed with sensual or intellectual pursuits, that he scarce has any power left for effective thought upon moral subjects. How fearfully some give way to worldly interests and claims, and others also to intellectual pursuits, some of you must know but too well.

Yet those moral wants you have neglected will some day arise and make their demands heard. It is well if they assume this urgency while yet their supply is possible. The prodigal son was a case of one who felt the pressure of these wants. He said, " I must go home to my father ". David entered on record his testimony, " My soul thirsteth for thee, my flesh longeth for thee in a dry and thirsty land, where no water is ". " As the hart panteth after the water brooks, so panteth my soul after thee, O God. My soul thirsteth for God, for the living God ; when shall I come and appear before God?" The mind thus becomes deeply conscious of cravings and aspirations which have God for their object, and which nothing but God can supply. If you examine the nature of these wants, you find them in part social. The mind craves communion with other minds. It thirsts for society, and wisely concludes that no society, no fellowship with other minds, can in any wise compare with communion with God. Perhaps he has tried the fellowship of mortals, and found it still unsatisfying. Hence he craves the richer, far richer, fellowship with the Father and with his Son Jesus Christ. He longs to rise above communion with the finite to hold communion with the Infinite. Weary of drawing instructions from erring man, he thirsts for the pure fountains of knowledge as they flow from the Infinite Intelligence. Conscious that he must himself exist for ever, he craves the acquaintance and sympathy of his eternal Maker and Father. As he comes to know something of his great and glorious Friend, he feels that he needs an eternity in which to study God in his multiform and wonderful works and ways. And when he comes to breathe the atmosphere of purity which invests the glorious Presence, how intensely does he long for deliverance from all moral corruption! Oh, how does his soul thirst for an ever-growing conformity to God! The language of holy men on the sacred page is exceedingly strong on these points, as we may see from David's Psalms and

Paul's Epistles. The latter declares, "Yea, doubtless, I count all things but loss for the excellency of the knowledge of Christ Jesus, my Lord ; for whom I have suffered the loss of all things, and do count them but dung, that I may win Christ and be found in him". No one can read these strong utterances of feeling, desire, and purpose, without seeing that the mind may develop itself with amazing intensity in this direction. There is scope and occasion for its utmost energies and aspirations.

CONCLUSION

1. He must be wretched who neglects to supply his physical wants. He must pay the stern penalty of his neglect, as he will soon learn to his sorrow. Each organ of the body needs its appropriate development, exercise, and nutriment. He who should disregard the laws of his constitution in respect to the proper supply of these constitutional demands will find, ere long, that the penalty of such neglect is fearful and sure.

In like manner, if he stultifies himself and takes no pains to inquire after truth and knowledge ; if he never troubles himself to know, and denies to his intellectual nature all its just demands, he must be far more wretched than a brute can be. But let a man neglect all spiritual culture and training, he becomes far more wretched still. Physical demands cease with the death of the body ; the spiritual must continue during his entire existence, stretching on and still on for ever, and probably for ever increasing.

2. How cruel for a man to consider himself as

merely a brute! Giving himself up to a grovelling life, regardless of his spiritual nature and even of his intellectual nature also, what a wretch he must be! Ye who are students know how to pity and how to despise him!—You can understand what he loses, for you know what satisfaction is taken in finding out the reasons of things. But see the mere animal who never looks abroad, never raises an inquiry. Why does he not set himself to study and think? Why not cast his thoughts abroad for knowledge? Why does he live a fool and a dunce, when he might be a *man?*

3. How cruel to treat anybody else as a mere animal! This is the most cruel thing you can do towards a fellow-being. You deny the existence of those great qualities which constitute him a man. You feed him as you would a horse, withholding all aliment for his intelligent mind. You feed him and your horse, each for the same reason;—you want to keep him in working order to serve your selfish purposes. You regard all knowledge beyond what your horse needs as only so much injury to him. Holding your slave as his master, do you send him to school? Never. Do you teach him to read? Never. Do you provide him any means of instruction? No. In the same manner you shut down the gate upon his moral nature. You close up the windows of his soul and keep it as utterly dark as possible to the light of heaven. You tighten the thumb-screws down on every inlet of knowledge, so that he shall never know that he is anything more or other than a beast! Is not this horrible? What, then,

shall we say of the man who does just this upon himself!

4. The more a man develops his intellectual faculties, yet neglects moral culture, the more miserable he
becomes. It is striking to see how wretched the most
highly cultivated men become. During all the latter
years of his life, Daniel Webster was never seen sober,
but he was wretched. While in his senses, his mind
was deep in sorrow. Look in upon Congress and see
there the great men of our land and of other lands;
not a man of them is happy without piety and sound
moral culture. Go and ask Byron if his gigantic mind
and almost superhuman genius, made him an angel
of bliss. Ask him if he found this world a paradise.
Perhaps no man ever cursed his fellow-beings more intensely, or enjoyed less in their society, than he. All such
men, with high intellectual culture, make themselves
wretched because they leave their moral powers in a
state of utter wreck and distortion. There is no escape
from this result. High intellectual culture must inevitably develop the idea and the claims of God. Let them
turn their inquiries which way they will, they find God,
and must feel more or less convicted of obligation to
love and obey them. Repelling these obligations, it is
impossible that they can be otherwise than wretched.
I alluded to the case of a young lawyer who asked,
"What makes me so unhappy? I feel myself thoroughly wretched, and surely I can see no reason for it."
The secret was this: all his life long he had neglected
God; his studies had more and more brought God
to view, and his sensibilities, under the action of

conscience, had become exceedingly acute. How could he be otherwise than wretched! He might not see the reason of his unhappy state; yet, if he had well considered the laws of his moral nature, he would have found the reason lying there. Many of you begin to find the same results in your experience, and you must realise them more and more if you remain alienated in heart from God while yet your intelligence is more and more revealing God and his rightful claims on your heart.

5. Neglecters of God are not well aware either of the cause or the degree of their wretchedness. The wants of their physical nature are all met. They are fed and clad, and have every comfort that their physical system craves. Their social wants, too, are met. They have friends and society. They have also cultivated taste and any desired amount of objects for its gratification. There is a library and books in plenty. There are works of art from the masters in every profession. What more could they need? Yet they are wretched. What is the matter? How many thousand times has this inquiry been made, What can be the matter with me? I have everything heart can wish, or the eye desire,—books, teachers, unbounded sources of information,—yet I am unhappy; what does ail me?

I can tell you what. There is another side of your nature, more important than all the rest, and more craving, yet you shut off all its demands, and deny its claims. You have a conscience, yet you resist its monitions. You have desires correlated to God, yet you deny them their appropriate gratification. No fact is more ennobling to human nature than this, that man has desires correlated to God even as he has to his fellow-men, so that he can no more be happy without God than he can be without the sympathy and society of man. We all understand this law of human nature. We see man thirsting for companionship with his fellow-man, longing for society, and we cannot fail to see and to say that man is so constructed in his very nature that he must have society. Deprive him of it and he is wretched. Now the striking fact is that man has an equally strong demand in his very constitution for sympathy and fellowship with God. Unless this too be supplied, he cannot be happy.

Suppose you were to meet a man as ignorant of his physical wants as most men are of their spiritual. He does not understand that he must have food for his stomach, clothes for his body, heat to warm him in the winter frosts. Ah! you would see the reason of his misery? Strange he does not know enough to supply his wants!

Or suppose him equally ignorant of his intellectual wants. He starves his soul of knowledge. Lean and barren, he seems to be panting for something higher and better, yet unaware both of the nature of this craving and of the proper source of supply. How easily could you tell him that "for the soul to be without knowledge is not good"!

So there is also a moral side to man's nature, and he can never be supremely happy till he becomes morally perfect. He struggles to get out of his moral agony ; feels as if he should die if he cannot get out from under this moral load. Who has not felt this loathing of his abominable self, because he did not and would not search after God! Never did any man long for food or water more intensely than the man who suffers himself to attend to the inner voice of his moral being, and thirsts after God.

6. Blessed are they who do hunger and thirst, for when they cry unto God to be filled, he will fill them. Let them cry unto God for bread and water; does he not hear their cry? Ah, verily,—he hears the young ravens when they cry, and the young lions when they roar and suffer hunger; and the infant voices of his intelligent creation are not less sure to come up into his ear. Does he not love to supply these wants which grow out of the nature he gave them? Indeed he does. He spread out the fair earth and its rich fields of lovely green. He meant to fill the earth with supplies for man and beast, yea, for every living thing.

In like manner, of the mental wants of his intelligent creatures. He loves to meet these with open hand;—loves to excite the spirit of inquiry and then supply to us the means of gratification. The things we need to know he loves to teach us.

But our moral and spiritual wants, he is infinitely more ready to supply. Does not your inner heart say, Verily, this must be so? It is so. No sooner does the soul go forth after God, than he is near—ineffably near. It is wonderful to see how soon God is found when once the soul begins in true earnest to inquire after him. Is it not striking that God should so love to reveal himself, and should take such pains to insinuate

himself into our confidence, and, as it were, work
himself into universal communion and contact with our
whole souls, so as to fill every moral want of our being?
In view of this desire and effort on his part, and in view
also of the means provided and promised for this result,
we can see why God should command us to "be filled
with the Spirit". Such infinite supplies provided, and
such earnest desire manifested on the part of God to
have us appropriate these supplies to their utmost extent;—it is as if an ocean of water were suspended above
our heads, and we have only to lift the valve and let down
these ocean waters upon our needy souls. There is
the promise, let down like a silken cord; what have we
to do but to take hold of it and pull down infinite
blessings!

7. Until man feels his spiritual wants, he will resist
all attempts you may make to bring him to God.
Hence the necessity of touching the mainspring of danger,—of arousing his fears, and developing his moral
sensibility. Hence the need of appeals to his conscience and to his sense of danger. Until you can make
his moral nature sensitive, and rouse up his dark and
dead soul to moral feelings, there is no hope for him.
But when you can touch this side of his nature, and
quicken him to feeling, and even to agony, under the
lash of conscience, and make him really appreciate his
wants, then he begins to feel his wants, and to ask how
they can be met and supplied. This is the true secret
of promoting revivals. You must go around among
these dark, insensible minds, and pour in light upon
this side of their nature. You must wake them up to

earnest thought—you must rouse up the man's conscience and soul till he shall cry out after God and his salvation.

I always have strong hopes of students; for although they sometimes get wise in their own conceits, and sometimes render themselves ridiculous by their low ambition, yet, taken as a class, there is great hope of them. If suitable means are used, very many of them will be converted. Probably no class of students ever passed through college, the right means of instruction and influence being used with them, without deeply feeling the power of truth, and many of them becoming converted. They must, almost of necessity, feel every blow that is struck; every truth, brought home clearly through their intelligence upon their conscience, wakens a response, and impels the soul to cry out after God. Hence I have strong hopes of you. Yet many of you, I know, are not now converted. God grant you may be soon! I hope the hearts of this Christian people will reach your case in strong effectual prayer. You can indeed resist every effort made to save you—if you will; you can reject Christ, however earnest his entreaties or tender his loving kindness; but you cannot change your nature so that it shall be happy in rebellion against God and his truth; you cannot hush the rebukes of an abused conscience for ever; these wants of your inner being must be met, or what will become of you? Your bodily wants will soon cease; and you need not care much therefore for them. Your intellectual pleasures, also, must ere long come to an end; for how can they pass over with you into the realm of outer darkness, where are weeping and wailing and gnashing of teeth! Doubtless that is a state not of light, and truth, and joy in pursuit of knowledge; but of delusions, and errors, and of knowledge agonising its possessor with keenest pangs for ever and ever! I do not believe sinners will have any intellectual pleasure in hell. It cannot be possible that they will enjoy any knowledge they will have there, or any means of attaining knowledge. The very idea is precluded by the relations that conscience must sustain to everything they know. All possible knowledge must have some bearing upon God, duty, and their moral relations, and hence must serve only to harrow up their sensibilities with keenest anguish. Oh, how will they gnash their teeth and gnaw their tongues in direst woe for ever! "There is no peace, saith my God, to the wicked!" More and more deeply dissatisfied to all eternity! Execrating and cursing their insane selves for the madness of rejecting God and his gospel when they might have had both, now it only remains for them to wail in bitterness and anguish, lifting up their unavailing cries, to which the thunders of Jehovah's curse respond in everlasting echoes, "Woe to the wicked; it shall be ill with him; for the reward of his hands shall be given him".

O sinner, will you yet press on into the very jaws of such a hell!